THE GRE

EUROPEAN AND AMERICAN LEADERS

IN GOG THEY TRUST?

BOOK I

Book I and Book II of *In Gog They Trust?* are based on the prophecies taken from *Daniel* and *The Revelation* which center around the coming **THREE-FOLD UNION** of the **people of modern-day Spiritualism**, the **Catholic Church**, and the **American apostate Protestants** of the United States whom Militant Islam is violently against. Book I is a brief overall picture showing why Muslim Militants today believe that it is the **International Order of Freemasonry** who are the main architects behind the establishment of the coming **Antichrist System**. Book I also has a brief overall view of Islam and Muhammad's confused version of the coming Antichrist (Dajjal) and Gog and Magog.

Book II is a full-length book of more than 350 pages loaded with footnotes and illustrations which continues to show, with overwhelming documented proof, how the **Freemasons** **infiltrated** both the **Vatican** and the **American Protestant churches** in an effort to **transform** their **CHURCHES** into **INTERFAITH CENTERS** in preparation for a grand merger of **Paganism, Roman Catholicism,** and **Protestantism** as predicted from Revelation 16:1-19. The author shows with plenty of documented evidence from Roman Catholic sources how **Pope John XXIII** and **Pope Paul VI** and **Pope John Paul II** were connected with Freemasonry's Masonic-based Illuminati Plan to globalize the whole world into a One-World Government with a One-World Religion, a One-World Monetary System, and a One-World Rest Day *via* the **United Nations**.

SIM & SONS' PUBLISHING HOUSE
Henderson, NV 89052

The Testimony from a Former New Age Illuminist

Back in 2001, the Lord Jesus Christ called me out. I was born into a family of Freemasons, who are cells of the Illuminati. This may be a term that you are not familiar with; yet, for generations, my family has been involved in Luciferian worship and doctrine. This is not something that I chose; this was something that, as my mother said to me, "This is what we are. This is what we have always been, and this is what we will continue to be. We don't know anything else."

Lucifer is known as the "Light Bearer;" and he camouflaged himself in ancient Mythology as "***ILU***," the **ILLUMINATED ONE**. However, in the Bible, he is **SATAN**. The word "***Illuminati***" derived from the name "***ILU***," which was the name given to the bright Sky-god whom Lucifer pretended to be among the ancient Chaldeans. This is the god of the Freemasons that is interwoven with the secret society of the Illuminati. I don't know how many generations of my family have been involved with Freemasonry. However, I know that the roots of my family tree go back to at least the time of Pope Clement V who had the Knights Templars put to death between A.D. 1307-1314. The Knights Templars is the 13th-Century term that the secret society of the Freemasons, with which my family is still very active, was using at this time in history.

From a child up, I sought to become clairvoyant through the practice of **YOGA** a.k.a. Transcendental Meditation. This practice involves opening up what is called in Occult circles "the Third Eye," which the Masonic Seal seen on the back of the American one-dollar bill is promoting. It was the Freemasons who placed this Occult symbol of the All-Seeing Eye there.

At age 12, I learned to levitate my body, move things around through astroprojection, and see things through the power of clairvoyance. This was something that I thought, at that time, was normal behavior. I would come home from school and go to my room for several hours and take a trip into the supernatural. First, I would go into my mantra and then find myself levitating off my bed and spending time in a world full of spirits, whom I thought, back then, were my dead Masonic ancestors. When I went to my parents and told them what I was up to, it wasn't abnormal to them. To them it was, "Be safe; be careful; watch out when you are out there."

After being led to study the Bible years later, I came to realize that the spirits with whom I had been communicating were actually devils in disguise! I was never shown what these forbidden practices of Illuminism were actually linked with until I was guided to read **Deuteronomy 18:9-13**. Please read what our Lord said about the Canaanites who were deeply involved in these sciences of the Occult in their day, for these warnings from this world's True God are just as pertinent to us now as they were to the ancient Jews. I know this to be true because this captive has been set free. There are modern-day Canaanites who are busy trying to overthrow the worship of the God of Abraham while, at the same time, pretending to be Christians. However, things began to change for me when a born-again Christian named Bobby Richardson came up to me at work and planted a seed in my mind which I didn't realize would grow into what it has today. Bobby said:

"**You don't know what you are running with, do you**?"

He kind of explained it to me and then gave me a couple of words that caused me to want to research into just what he was pointing to. As I began to research what these two words meant, I ended up reading material written by Wil Sutton, who is the author of several Christ-centered books about the Antichrist and also about the rise and evolution of the Masonic-based Order of the Illuminati. It was Wil Sutton's books that opened my eyes to a greater amount of knowledge about the deceptions of modern-day Spiritualism of which I had been a victim. As a result, I am now a brand plucked out of the fire and a loyal follower of the Lamb of God that taketh away the sins of the world.

Your Brother in Christ Jesus,
Mark Cleminson

AUTHOR'S PREFACE

My Jewish, Christian, Muslim, and New Age reader, I have been a student of the **SCIENCE** of Archaeology, ancient History, ancient Mythology, and the ancient prophecies found in the books of *Daniel* and *The Revelation* for about 34 years now. I have also been a diligent student of all your religions. In 1970, I wondered, "If we have One God, then why do we have so many different religions which all claim to have been founded by God but, at the same time, have started their own separate World Revolutions in an effort to violently overthrow each other?" Is God a God of confusion? Have you ever felt like saying, "Will the real God stand up?" Well, in 1970, I did; and it was at this time that this independent researcher turned from what the **CLERGY** of these world religions have taught about God and began his own research to find out who God was, is, and is to come.

First, I wanted to prove to myself that there was a God and that the Judeo-Christian Bible is the inspired Word of God that it claims to be. I wanted to see if what Moses wrote in the book of Genesis about Creation, the Flood, and the Tower of Babel could be proven through the Natural Sciences of Archaeology and ancient History.

In the meantime, I also wanted to discover where all these pagan religions first developed and how our ancient ancestors were fooled into worshipping these false gods and goddesses by their own clergy of their day. It was also in the early 1970s that this writer first began to study about Freemasonry and the prophecies about Muhammad and Islam from Revelation, Chapter 9. After all these years of research, I have come to the conclusion that what Jesus predicted in Revelation 12:9 about **SATAN** deceiving the whole world is not to be taken lightly by any of us. I offer **NO APOLOGIES** to the **PRIESTS** of Catholicism, **PASTORS** of mainstream Christianity, **SHAYKHS** and/or **MULLAHS** of Islam, or the **ADEPTS** of Freemasonry for what I am exposing in any of my fully-documented publications. However, this writer takes no joy in exposing these truths to them or to any of my readers, but that all of us will repent and be found on the True God's side on Judgment Day.

BAHRAIN AUSTRALIA ARGENTINA TURKEY UNITED ARAB EMIRATES SYRIA SPAIN

OPERATION DESERT STORM

On August 2, 1990 Iraq invaded the country of Kuwait. In response to the aggression of Saddam Hussein, a United Nations Coalition was formed to ensure the liberation of Kuwait and thusly, OPERATION DESERT SHIELD was born. Upon Iraq failing to meet the United Nations January 15, 1991 deadline for withdrawal, Allied Forces joined together to begin OPERATION DESERT STORM.

Let It Be Known That

BM3 LANCE M. ZORTMAN

was a participant in OPERATION DESERT STORM and by this participation aided in the liberation of Kuwait and the promotion of President George Bush's "New World Order."

Commanding Officer

THE GREAT APOSTASY OF EUROPEAN AND AMERICAN LEADERS... IN GOG THEY TRUST?

To your left, you will see an award that former President Bush, Sr. gave a Marine for his efforts to help liberate Kuwait from Saddam Hussein in the first Gulf War. The writer met this ex-Marine, and the bravery of our military men and women who fought in the Gulf Wars is without question. However, what is in question is what is written under Lance's name. Here, George Bush, Sr. openly admits that he is promoting the Occult-based *NEW WORLD ORDER*, which actually began on May Day, 1776. Most Americans today really do not have the slightest clue why Muslim suicide commandos conducted a devastating attack on New York and Washington on September 11, 2001. The reader may be very surprised to discover that all this terrible carnage that the Muslim fanatics have caused has its roots in what Muhammad interpreted from the prophecies found in the Bible about the **ANTICHRIST** and also what was written in the *KORAN* about an ancient **WALL** known as **GOG** and **MAGOG** that was built on the southwestern shore of the Caspian Sea in an effort to keep out the Scythians (Magogites) from entering into the Middle East. In this book, the reader will be made aware that there is a dangerous bloody conflict between the leaders of militant Islam and the adepts of the international Order of Freemasonry. Much of the slaughter of mankind from the 6th Century A.D. onward has been caused by the leaders of the Papacy, the Muslims, and the Knights Templars (Freemasons) over who is going to control the Holy Land and the world. Although the Papacy and the Freemasons became deadly enemies after A.D. 1307, they are now, in the 21st Century, fusing together with mainstream Protestant Christianity in an effort to bring about a New World Order, which these Muslim Militants are violently against.

Through His apostle John, **JESUS** warned His loyal followers that in our day a WORLD FEDERATION, which He called "**BABYLON THE GREAT**" (Revelation 17:5; see also 16:19; 18:21), will be formed against the **GOD** of Abraham and His people. This coming World Federation was foretold in the *BOOK OF REVELATION* to be eventually formed by three world powers that JESUS symbolized as the DRAGON, the BEAST, and the FALSE PROPHET. (See Revelation 16:13-19) (See diagram in the back of this book)

JESUS warned in the *BOOK OF REVELATION* that, in these Last Days, it would be SATAN who will unite the world into this coming **WORLD FEDERATION** which will oppress those who stay loyal to Him and refuse to join it. This coming **WORLD FEDERATION** will be an alliance of **international MERCHANTS, ARTISANS, MUSICIANS,** and **RELIGIOUS** and **POLITICAL LEADERS** of the nations of our AGE. In Revelation 18:23, it is predicted that these conspirators against GOD and His people will be considered to be the most honored men and women of the world. They are a league of this world's **RULING CLASSES**, whom JESUS foretold in Revelation 18:23 would be connected with the deceptions of SORCERY, "*for by thy **SORCERIES** were all nations deceived.*"

Back in 1980, I published *Beware It's Coming - The Antichrist 666*. It was my first book, and I wanted to show my readers how we today can, indeed, actually prove the literal truth of the Judeo-Christian Bible and its prophecies through the NATURAL SCIENCES, such as Archaeology, ancient History, and Anthropology. Not only does this book prove to my Jewish and Muslim reader, without any doubt, that JESUS of Nazareth fulfilled, to the letter, every Old Testament prophecy that foretold the coming Messiah, but this volume also shows my Jewish, Muslim, and Christian reader how we can tell the difference between the **CHRIST** and the **ANTICHRIST**. It clearly shows from Bible prophecy how this "***SPIRIT OF ANTICHRIST***" (See 1 John 4:3) would first establish a system and then "***THAT ANTICHRIST SHALL COME***." (See 1 John 2:18) It is in this volume that we will also take a journey through the Science of Archaeology and discover where Baal Worship and that mysterious number of doom 666 actually derived from and who is branded with it today.

Later, in 1983, I published another volume entitled *The New Age Movement and The Illuminati 666*. This volume is centered in the prophecies about how the people of modern-day **Spiritualism** would end up controlling the political and financial institutions of the world through **Occult-based secret societies**, such as Freemasonry; the Illuminati; the Rosicrucians; the Theosophical Society; the Rockefeller-founded Council on Foreign Relations, who were the founders of the United Nations; and the Bilderberg Group, who are the braincenter of these advocates who are trying to bring the whole world under a New World Order. The reader will discover with plenty of documented proof seen in this volume that these branches of the **New Age** and **New World Order Movements** first started as a **Masonic-based World Revolution** to eventually overthrow all religions and all governments after the year A.D. 2000. This plan to take over the entire world by using the LODGES of **FREEMASONRY** was first launched from Bavaria, Germany, at the founding of the dangerous secret society of the **Illuminati** by Professor Adam Weishaupt on **May 1, 1776.**[1]

Ironically enough, the motto for this Masonic-based World Revolution is seen on the back of the American one-dollar bill under the pyramid. "***NOVUS ORDO SECLORUM***," which is in Latin, means "***New Order for the Ages***" a.k.a. ***New World Order***.[2] This writer discovered years ago that everything that these dangerous Occult-based secret societies, like **FREEMASONRY** and the **ILLUMINATI**, believe and promote has originated from the Chaldean religion of Astrology. Lower-ranking Masons do not realize what they are linked with.

According to the *Compleat Astrologer*, the religion of Astrology teaches that mankind will pass through **SIX AGES** and the **SEVENTH** was to begin after the year A.D. 2000; and among people of modern-day Spiritualism, it is known as the ***Age of Aquarius*** a.k.a. the ***Golden Age***.[3] The term "***ILLUMINATI***" was used in Europe before the secret society of the Illuminati of Bavaria was first founded on May Day, 1776. The name *Illuminati* was given to the adepts of Occultism, specifically to those who were quite learned or who possessed light from direct communication with supernatural or so-called higher intelligences. Illuminism or the Illuminati were also associated with Occult-based secret societies, like the Knights Templars and their successors, the Freemasons; the Rosicrucians; the Martinists; the Ordo Templi Orientis (O.T.O.), with which the infamous Aleister Crowley was connected; and also the Theosophical Society that was co-founded by a 19th-Century Luciferian named Helena P. Blavatsky. It was Blavatsky's successor Annie Besant and Gandhi who led the Theosophical Society

The origin of the New Age Movement derived from the slogan on the back of the United States one-dollar bill:

Novus Ordo Seclorum

(New Order of the Ages / Age of Aquarius)

The seven ages of mankind according to Astrology:

10000 - 8000 BC BC	8000 - 6000 BC BC	6000 - 4000 BC BC	4000 - 2000 BC BC	2000 - 0 BC	0 - 2000 AD	2000 AD
THE AGE OF **LEO**	THE AGE OF **CANCER**	THE AGE OF **GEMINI**	THE AGE OF **TAURUS**	THE AGE OF **ARIES**	THE AGE OF **PISCES**	THE AGE OF **AQUARIUS**

in their efforts to overthrow both Christianity and the British Government in India.[4] According to the advocates of this Masonic-based New Age and New World Order Revolution, Christianity shall be replaced by modern-day Spiritualism a.k.a. Mysticism during their coming ***Age of Aquarius***. However, the Biblical JESUS has other plans.

This diagram to your left shows how New Age beliefs are rooted and grounded in the religion of Astrology. According to New Age thinking, **JESUS** was the Christ who ushered in the ***Age of Pisces*** (0 - A.D. 2000) and the Christian Dispensation. However, another christ was to come (not to be confused with the Biblical JESUS) to usher in the ***Age of Aquarius*** whose name is **MAITREYA**.[5] We shall see more about the New Age messiah later. As we shall see, it is not by chance that the secret society of **FREEMASONRY** chose the year **1776** to launch their Occult-based **World Revolution** against Christianity and all religions and governments. If the reader will look on the back of the American ONE-DOLLAR bill, you will see a MASONIC SEAL. At the base of the Egyptian pyramid, you will see **1776** in ROMAN NUMERALS.

Has the reader ever wondered why there is an Egyptian pyramid on the back of the American ONE-DOLLAR bill with the All-Seeing Eye of the Egyptian god ***AMEN-RA*** displayed there? Doesn't it say "**IN GOD WE TRUST**?" Just what GOD are the Rothschilds, who own over 50% of the stock in the Federal Reserve System, talking about here? Weren't the Egyptians in Moses' day great enemies of the Hebrew God and did not this same GOD bury the Pharaoh and his army in the Red Sea? Then why do we have in Protestant America a currency which exalts the Chaldean, Egyptian, and Roman Sky-gods?

Just before the GOD of Israel punished the ancient JEWS for blending **BAAL WORSHIP** into the worship of the Hebrew God, our Lord told Jeremiah the prophet that there was a **CONSPIRACY** among the **leaders of ISRAEL** to overthrow HIM. The quote about this is seen in the illustration on the next page. It is very eye-opening for sleepy-eyed Christians of the United States to discover that there is also a **CONSPIRACY** among us within the United States, as well, to overthrow the worship of ***ELOHIM*** and replace Him with ***BAAL*** in this country.

It should be noted here that the warnings about this coming **World Federation** found in Chapters 14, 16, 17, and 18 of the *BOOK OF REVELATION* were originally written in the Greek language. This

"And the Lord said unto me, A ***CONSPIRACY*** *is found among the men of Judah, and among the inhabitants of Jerusalem.*

"They are ***TURNED BACK*** *to the* ***iniquities*** *of their* ***FOREFATHERS****, which* ***REFUSED*** *to hear my words; and they went after other* ***GODS*** *to serve them: the house of Israel and the house of Judah have* ***broken my covenant*** *which I made with their fathers.*

"Therefore thus saith the Lord, Behold, ***I will bring evil upon them****, which they shall not be able to escape; and though they shall cry unto me, I will not hearken unto them."*

Jeremiah 11:9-11

*Amazingly, the word "****CONSPIRACY****" in Greek adds to the very year the* ***SECRET SOCIETY*** *of the* ***ILLUMINATI*** *launched their* ***Occult Revolution*** *on the* ***DRUID*** *festival of* ***BELTANE (MAY DAY)****.*

ΣΥΝΩΜΟΣΕΙΑ

200 400 50 800 40 70 200 5 10 1 = 1776

TAKEN FROM *THE 21ST-CENTURY REVELATION SEMINAR TEACHER'S MANUAL*, WILLIAM JOSIAH SUTTON

illustration to your left was taken from *The 21st-Century Revelation Seminar Teacher's Manual*. It is showing how the word "***CONSPIRACY***," when written in the Greek language and added in its numerical values, will add to the number **1776.**[6]

I learned about this when I came to a website that showed the Greek alphabet and its numerical values. I learned over 20 years ago that the number **666** originally derived from the **Zodiac**, as seen on page 22 of this book; how JESUS' name, when written in Greek, will add to **888**; how the Chaldean god **TEITAN**, whom **SATAN** was worshipped as, adds to **666**; and how both the Pope and the Papacy are branded with this number.[7] However, I was, indeed, taken by surprise when this same website showed that both the names "**EUROPE**" and "**NEW YORK**," when translated into the Greek language, will add to **666**. (See Book II of *In Gog They Trust?*) This absolutely amazed me because I have been showing, since 1971, how secret societies from **Europe** and **America** are bringing about this coming World Federation that JESUS called in Revelation, Chapter 17, "BABYLON THE GREAT!"

These eye-opening facts about the **Masonic Revolution**, which is bringing about a ***NOVUS ORDO SECLORUM***; how the word "***CONSPIRACY***" in Greek adds to **1776**; and how the names "**EUROPE**" and "**NEW YORK**" in Greek add to 666 may have brought a chuckle among my Muslim militant readers whose clerics are presently teaching their followers that the **RULING CLASSES** of **EUROPE** and **AMERICA** are modern **GOG** and **MAGOG**. Muslim scholars, as we shall see, are also following the prophecies about the **ANTICHRIST** in the Bible, but have their own version about how the world will be brought under an Antichrist System and who this **ANTICHRIST** is that will appear. We will see from their own words why Muslim scholars believe that Jews and Christians from Britain and the United States are the people today who make up **GOG** and **MAGOG** who were foretold in the *BOOK OF REVELATION* to lead the world into the **Battle of Armageddon** because of their Frankish and Masonic connections.[8]

Today, learned Muslims are spreading that the early Frankish tribes, who founded Gaul and the British Isles, and the Royal Bloodline of the Merovingian Dynasties of Europe were all descendants of King **MAGOG**, the son of **JAPHETH**, who first settled in what is now known as southern **Russia** (Scythia). (See Genesis 10:2) History shows that Muslims during the **First Crusade** (1095-1099) fought against the **Merovingian Knights of Europe** in their quest to take back the city of Jerusalem from the Muslims who conquered it in A.D. 638. At the head of these Merovingian Knights, there was **Godfroi de Bouillon** who, in **1090**, founded in Jerusalem a Gnostic-based secret society of the **Priory of Zion** about nine years before the First Crusade began in Jerusalem. The **Priory of Zion** is where the **Knights Templars** derived in **1118-1307**, and this society became the **Scottish Rite of Freemasonry** in England under **King James VI of Scotland** (1567-1603), who united England under his reign. The Merovingian King James VI of Scotland became King James I of England.[9]

The name "***Merovingian***" derived from a complete fable of Gnostic heresy that was invented by them in the 1st Century. **Gnosticism** is a blend of Babylonian witchcraft with elements of Christian beliefs which can be traced to **Simon the SORCERER** who wanted to buy the gifts of the Holy Spirit with money. Gnosticism is still centered in the forbidden practice of **YOGA** and **NECROMANCY**, which is invoking supernatural spirits in an effort through certain rituals to gain esoteric knowledge and/or power from them. The secret society of the **Priory of Zion**, to which **Freemasonry** can be traced today, was a LODGE where the mystics and/or gurus of Hinduism, Zoroastrianism, Cabalism, Gnosticism, and Islamic Mysticism (Sufism) of that day congregated to share their mystical knowledge.

The Gnostic Christians claimed JESUS was never crucified and that **Mary Magdalene married JESUS and had children**, one of whom was supposedly called "***MEROVEE***," from which the name **Merovingian** derived. Gnosticism teaches that **Mary Magdalene**, being pregnant with child, fled with Joseph of Arimathea, the apostle Philip, and a boat loaded with Christians to the southern shore of France, where she gave birth to JESUS' son, **Merovee**. Even though there is not five words of truth in this Gnostic doctrine, nevertheless, there was a **spurious Royal Dynasty of Frankish kings of Europe** that was founded on this fable, which is still with us today. It was in southern France that the **Merovingian Royal Bloodline** of the **House of David** started, from which both **Queen Elizabeth II** of the **House of Windsor** and also the late **Princess Diana** of the **House of Stuart derived**.[10]

England's Royal Dynasty was, indeed, founded by Freemasons who were formerly Knights Templars. Today, **Queen Elizabeth II** is called the "**Patron of Freemasonry**," and today English Freemasons still believe that the Merovingian Dynasty is extremely important because they think this Royal Bloodline is divine. There are not a few today, who know the real issues of the day and who have been studying the prophecies from the Bible about the **Antichrist**, who believe that **Prince William**, the son of **Charles** and **Diana** who is presently being groomed to take the throne of England, will be the long-expected Antichrist. However, this writer does not believe that the **SEAT of the Antichrist System** is in jolly old England, but within the city which is surrounded by **SEVEN HILLS**. (See Revelation 13:18; 17:9)

We will look more into this counterfeit **Royal House of the Merovingian Dynasty** later, but let's see some more of what the Muslim revolutionaries today think about all of this. Muslim militants use the history behind the Merovingian Dynasties of Europe to show how the **British** and **American Freemasons** are trying to set up the **headquarters** of this coming **New World Order** in **modern-day Israel**. As we shall see, Muslim fanatics today tie in the modern descendants of the **Khazar Jews of Russia** (A.D. 650-1016) as being directly related to Freemasonry and Zionism and the people who make up **GOG** and **MAGOG** in these Last Days.[11] A complete and fully-documented study about how the **Frankish KINGS of Europe** can, indeed, be traced in the Bible, the Science of Archaeology, and History back to Japheth's son **Magog** is presented in Book II of *In Gog They Trust?*

Muslims were told by **Muhammad** that the **ANTICHRIST** will be a **white man** with **bushy hair** and **crooked legs** and will be **blind in one eye**.[12] Hence, the Masonic Seal seen on the back of the American ONE-DOLLAR bill, which is showing the **ONE EYE** over the pyramid, only helps seal Muslim fanatics' belief that it is the international Order of **Freemasonry** which is presently establishing the **Antichrist System** in the 21st Century.[13]

While investigating the origin of Freemasonry back in the 70s, I discovered the true origin of these mystical seals seen on the back of the American ONE-DOLLAR bill and how, indeed, the United States was founded in **1776** by men who were high-ranking **Freemasons** and/or Rosicrucians, whose greatest apostle was a Merovingian Knight named **Sir Francis Bacon** who was born in London in 1561 and died in 1626. He served under Queen Elizabeth I as Lord Keeper of Seal, and when she died in 1603, Bacon continued to serve the British government under the Merovingian King James I who also made him his **chancellor** until Bacon was charged with bribery and found guilty by his own admission in 1621.[14] However, no one in the 17th Century did more to spark the 18th-Century **Merovingian/Masonic Revolution** by pen and voice in an effort to eventually take over the entire world than this Merovingian Knight **Sir Francis Bacon**. This 17th-Century WIZARD made his way as a prolific Gnostic writer. It was his adventuresome tale, *New Atlantis*, which inspired the 18th-Century **Masons** and **Rosicrucians** to establish their Occult Revolution in the **New World**. The Masonic Revolution is based in the notion to bring about **Plato's Dream** of re-establishing the Socialist government of **Atlantis** worldwide. These Masonic seals on the American one-dollar bill are mystically revealing what their plans and purposes are.

For some 200 years before the founding of the United States, **AMERICA** was a haven for fleeing, European, Protestant Christians who were running for their very lives from fanatical Roman Catholic priests and inquisitors. The **Papacy** burned Europeans at the stake or put **Protestants** to the sword who refused to recognize the **Pope of Rome** as the **Vicarius Filii Dei,**[15] which is in Latin, and means "**Vicar of the Son of God**." Reader, the bloodstained pages of history show that the Roman Catholic Church, the Muslims, and the Freemasons all started their own **World Revolutions** in an effort to bring the people of this world under their own religious and political dictatorships.

The Roman Catholic clergy started their World Revolution to force the world to come under their power after **Clovis I** of Gaul (France) united the rivaling Frankish Merovingian kings of France and Germany under the subordination of the **Pope of Rome** by **A.D. 508.**[16] After destroying the last three Arian nations of the Vandals, Heruli, and the Ostrogoths who stood in her way, in **A.D. 538** the **Papacy** proclaimed herself the **Corrector of Heretics**[17] and began her long slaughter of Europeans who dared to challenge her authority, however, not without opposition. In A.D. 570, **Muhammad** was born, and his Muslim warriors became her greatest rival during the Middle Ages.

It is true that the **Freemasons**, since **1776**, have been controlling the political and financial destinies of America. Nevertheless, my Muslim reader, it will also be from **AMERICA** where a great Christian awakening about the rivaling **Papal, Masonic,** and **Muslim Revolutions** will finally come to **light again** starting in America's Northeast States. Much of this was first exposed back in the early part of the 19th Century in Northeast America by the **Anti-Masonic Movement** and also by the **Millerites** of the **1844 Movement**. About four years before the Masonic-based **Order of Skull & Bones** was founded at Yale University in **1832**, the *Wayne Sentinel* newspaper of western New York wrote what the **MASONIC REVOLUTION** had caused in Europe. The following quote is from the *Wayne Sentinel,* September 26, 1828:

> *"If you listen to the party which lately welcomed Don Miguel as their 'tutelar angel,' . . . the* ***Freemasons*** *have been the cause of all the 'seditions, privy conspiracies, and rebellions,' which, for the last thirty years have afflicted* ***Europe****. . . . The* ***Freemasons*** *are, therefore, radically and essentially, demagogues,* ***Jacobins****, conspirators, assassins, infidels, traitors, and ATHEISTS. Their BAND of union is formed of the broken cement of existing order - their* ***secret*** *is the watchword of sedition and rebellion - their object is* ***ANARCHY*** *and* ***PLUNDER*** *- . . . unless they are suppressed, there will soon be neither religion, morals, literature, nor civilized society left!"*

This writer has been investigating **Freemasonry** and its history since 1971, and what the *Wayne Sentinel* newspaper stated back in 1828 about Freemasonry is a historical fact. However, what the *Wayne Sentinel* failed to mention is what the **PAPAL** and **MUSLIM Revolutionaries** have been up to, as well. All of this is completely covered and documented within the seven volumes shown in the back of this book. There is now **another spiritual awakening** stirring in the Northeast States of America about the prophecies of *Daniel* and *The Revelation* and how they clearly predicted the **Papal, Muslim,** and **Masonic World Revolutions**, which have deeply affected the whole world. The sins of modern Babylon will surely be laid wide open to show us how this **Angel** from the **Bottomless Pit** has been deceiving the whole world through his human agents. As we take a deeper look at what Muhammad says about the Antichrist, we will see how *ISLAM's* founder's name, when placed in the Greek language, will also add to **666** and how Muslims are unwittingly being conditioned to accept the Antichrist!

At the beginning of 2004, this writer was also made aware of another astonishing move by these modern-day Nimrods of the United States to exalt themselves, like this first Mason of the Land of Shinar did in his day. I received a phone call from Mark Cleminson, who wrote the Introduction page to this book, about the proposed **FREEDOM TOWER** that will replace the destroyed World Trade Center in New York City, which is at the center of World Commerce today. Mark, who makes his home in New Hampshire, pointed out to me that this **Freedom Tower** will be the tallest building on earth, and it will be **1776** feet tall! Upon hearing about this, I immediately went to an Internet news website to see if what Mark said to me was true or not. Sure enough, it is true. This **Freedom Tower** will rise **1776** feet above Manhattan. This new SKYSCRAPER caught the interest of Mark, especially, because he was raised in a family of high-ranking Freemasons.

Mark and his wife grew up as children within the New Age Movement, whose secret and ultimate goal is to overthrow Biblical Christianity. Mark himself, from a child up, was deeply into the forbidden practices of **YOGA** and **NECROMANCY** and other **New Age** practices. Mark was actually a **SHAMAN** who often levitated in the air when practicing **YOGA** as he sought communication from **supernatural spirits** who were, in reality, **SATAN** and his **fallen angels**. He has related to me what these beings looked like. However, Mark never realized that these **supernatural beings**, with whom he communicated, were the **FALLEN ANGELS**, because the Bible was not taught at his home. However, back in 2001, Mark obtained the first two volumes of my books and, after reading them, he ended up swapping **New Age Shamanism** for **Biblical Christianity**! We have become friends now and co-workers in the Loud Cry of the Third Angel. (See Revelation, Chapters 14 and 18.) Mark is truly an example of what the **power of Jesus Christ** can do for those who learn to recognize His voice and obey it. Mark is now currently being asked by pastors of churches to come and give his testimony about how he was delivered by the power of the **SPIRIT OF CHRIST** from these demons of **ILLUMINISM** and how **JESUS** is now controlling things in his human **TEMPLE**.

It is interesting to note, in passing, that the **1776-foot-tall Freedom Tower**, that shall arise out of the ashes of **Ground Zero**, that Mark pointed out to me is being compared to the mythical firebird who has arisen out of its ashes only to become more powerful.[18] The EAGLE seen in the Masonic Seal is the Mason's version of the great Thunderbird of ancient Astrology, who is known as the **PHOENIX**. In the ancient Phoenician myth, the **PHOENIX** was the great Sun-bird who carried the souls of the dead to inhabit the STARS and the planets. The **PHOENIX** was said to have built a pyre of wood where he burned himself to ashes, only to arise out of the flames as an eternal powerful Sun-bird.[19]

Reader, this Masonic ***NOVUS ORDO SECLORUM*** is based in this myth about the **PHOENIX**. The adepts of Freemasonry, as well as the children of the New Age Movement that Freemasonry conceived, believe that before their ***Age of Aquarius*** is ushered in, the present world must be cleansed of all unenlightened people who refuse to join their **New Age Revolution**. New Age GURUS look to the year **A.D. 2000** as the "***Dawning of the Age of Aquarius***" and their brethren have been preaching, since the 18th Century, that complete **ANARCHY** must break out worldwide if Mother Earth is to survive. However, according to **New Agers**, out of the ashes of the nations of the world will come forth a New Planetary Order or a **New Atlantis**, as some call it. Amazingly, the Masonic brethren have a revolutionary slogan written in Latin to remind them of their ultimate goals. The Latin slogan is "***ORDO AB CHAO***" which means "***ORDER OUT OF CHAOS***."[20]

These 18th-Century Masonic/Illuminati conspirators planned to gain control of the financial and political destinies of the world by first uniting the American colonies into a **UNITED STATES** and then use this country to eventually unite the whole world under the subordination of Freemasonry's secret priesthood. As the **PHOENIX** burnt himself on a pyre of wood only to arise out of it as a new eternal bird, so did these 18th-Century adepts of Freemasonry plan to cause "***ORDO AB CHAO***" or "***ORDER OUT OF CHAOS***." Ironically enough, these are the very words which George W. Bush publicly stated when he first viewed the destruction of the World Trade Center by Muslim fanatics in New York City back on **9/11/2001**.

Albert G. Mackey

When a Freemason reaches the 33°, he is presented with this medallion. Masons are determined to bring about a New World Order and a mystical Universal Brotherhood. This is to be brought about by causing the present political, religious, and economic systems to collapse worldwide. Then, out of this chaos will arise a New World Order. This is seen in the motto of this 33° medallion, which is written in Latin. It says "Ordo Ab Chao" which means "Order out of Chaos."

"The reverse of the Great Seal depicts a Masonic emblem because more than 50 of the signatories of the Declaration of Independence were either Masons or Rosicrucians and were much concerned with the esoteric sciences such as astrology, numerology, tarot, Kabalah, etc. Benjamin Franklin and Thomas Jefferson were expert astrologers."

The Occult Illustrated Dictionary, Harvey Day, Kay & Ward, pp. 56, 57, Oxford University Press, NY, 1976

The two most sought-after scholars of Freemasonry in the 19th Century were **Albert Pike**, 33°, and **Albert G. Mackey**, 33°. To your left, you will see a photograph of Albert G. Mackey, 33°. Mackey is well-known in Masonic circles for his volumes entitled *The Encyclopaedia of Freemasonry and Its Kindred Sciences* and his many volumes about *The History of Freemasonry*. This illustration to your left was taken from *The 21st-Century Revelation Seminar Teacher's Manual*. In the photograph of Mackey, 33°, you will see a Masonic **jewel** on his jacket and within it is the Latin motto, ***Ordo Ab Chao***, which is an old Masonic Revolutionary slogan. Today, there is even in the modern State of Israel a Masonic Lodge of the **33°** which uses the Latin motto ***ORDO AB CHAO*** for the name of their **Supreme Council**. At the bottom, there is a quote which plainly states that the mysterious-looking **SEAL** on the back of the American one-dollar bill is, indeed, a Masonic emblem and that more than **50** of the signatories of the Declaration of Independence were either Masons or Rosicrucians.

Very few American Christians know that **Benjamin Franklin** himself was a Grand Master of Freemasonry and, besides being a convinced **DEIST** who rejected JESUS as the Son of God and Saviour of the world, **Franklin** was an **EXPERT ASTROLOGER**, as was **Thomas Jefferson**. The religion of Astrology is the worship of the Sun, Moon, and stars, instead of the God who really created them. The God of the Judeo-Christian Bible warns what will happen to all **Astrologers** and those who trust in them and those who refuse to repent and turn away from it. The following quote is taken from Isaiah 47:13, 14:

> *"Thou art wearied in the multitude of thy counsels. Let now the **ASTROLOGERS**, the **STARGAZERS**, the monthly **PROGNOSTICATORS**, stand up, and save thee from these things that shall come upon thee. Behold, they shall be as stubble; the **FIRE** shall burn them; they shall not deliver themselves from the **POWER OF THE FLAME**."*

Within this set of seven volumes, which are seen in the back of this book, there is page after page of archaeological and historical evidence which proves to its reader that everything that **SATAN** has

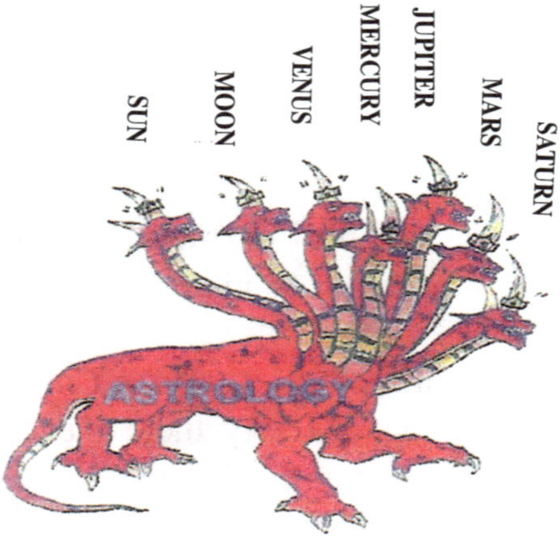

THE ZODIAC

6	32	3	34	35	1
7	11	27	28	8	30
19	14	16	15	23	24
18	20	22	21	17	13
25	29	10	9	26	12
36	5	33	4	2	31

This is an ancient astrological chart showing the numbers of the 36 divisions of the Zodiac. Any way these numbers are added together, they will add to the number of doom 666. However, in pagan Oriental thinking, the number 666 is an omen of good fortune.

1
2
3
4
5
6
7
8
9
10
11
12
13
14
15
16
17
18
19
20
21
22
23
24
25
26
27
28
29
30
31
32
33
34
35
36
666

used to deceive mankind, since the days of **Nimrod** unto our present day, has come to us from the Chaldean religion of Astrology. Astrology is the cornerstone of all the precepts found among the various divisions of both ancient and modern Spiritualism in which the **Papacy**, **Islam**, and **Freemasonry** are also rooted and grounded. To your left, you will see an illustration taken from the book, *The 21st-Century Revelation Seminar Teacher's Manual.* It is showing that the **number of doom (666)**, that Christians had better not be identified with in these Last Days, also derived from the religion of Astrology. Even the symbol of the **SEVEN-HEADED DRAGON**, which our Saviour used in Revelation, Chapters 12 and 13, to display in prophecy that **Old Serpent**, the **Devil** and **Satan**, was actually taken from the religion of Astrology to expose to us what this **GREAT DECEIVER** has done to mankind. In the book, *Origins of Astrology*, Lindsay, Barnes and Noble, Inc., 1971, pp. 375, 233, the following quote shows that even **ASTROLOGERS** themselves freely admit that the symbol of the **SEVEN-HEADED SERPENT** was the ancient symbol of Astrology:

> *"The **SERPENT** was a symbol of the planetary system in Astrology. The **SIX SPHERES OR SIX HEADS** stand for the **SIX PLANETS** with the **SERPENT ITSELF AS THE SUN**."*

> *"The seven planets: **SATURN, SUN, MOON, MARS, MERCURY, JUPITER** AND **VENUS**."*

These seven planets of the **Zodiac** were worshipped by our ancient ancestors as seven gods and/or goddesses that serpentine their way around the 360° circle of the Zodiac. Under them, there were 36 lesser gods stationed 10° apart around the Zodiac. Also, this illustration shows an astrological chart that ancient Astrologers used to predict the future by the use of mathematics. As shown, the numbers in the columns in this astrological chart are from 1-36 and if you add the numbers it shows us where the number of doom originated. Ironically enough, among the people of modern Mysticism today, this number 666 is not symbolizing a number of doom, as Christians see it, but of good fortune. It was the sacred number of the Chaldeans of southern Babylonia, from whom the Sumerians and their descendants, the Phoenician **SEA TRADERS**, borrowed. Jesus predicted that the religious leader who becomes the head of modern BABYLON THE GREAT will be branded with it. (See Revelation 13:18) JESUS warned that in the "**Time of the End**" there would appear **THREE WORLD POWERS** symbolized as the Dragon, the Beast, and the False Prophet (Revelation 16:13-16) who would at first be deadly enemies and then later would fuse together into a short-lived World Federation which would be divided into **TEN DIVISIONS**.

JESUS warned us nearly 2000 years ago that this coming **WORLD FEDERATION** will have such a control on the world that those who refuse to join it will not be able to **BUY or SELL**. The seven volumes of books seen in the back of this book show with overwhelming evidence that these **THREE WORLD POWERS** to your right are also symbolizing **THREE BEASTS** (See Revelation 11:7; 17:3, 8-17; 13:1-18) who have been identified as the people of modern **Spiritualism**, the **Papacy**, and the **American apostate Protestants** who are uniting today into **one common religion** through Interfaith Movements.

The book, *The New Age Movement and The Illuminati 666*, shows without any doubt that **Freemasonry** is rooted and grounded in the religion of Astrology. Masons who attend church are usually **Protestants** and among them we can find America's ruling class, like the **Rockefeller Family**, who have for years been establishing agencies to bring the world into a coming **World Federation**. Let's read together now from Revelation 13:16-18 what **JESUS** predicted through His apostle John about this last **superpower** of our day and how it will be this power who will be foremost in helping the **Pope of Rome** become the head of this coming **World Federation**.

> "*And he causeth all, both small and great, rich and poor, free and bond, to receive a **MARK** in their right hand, or in their foreheads: And that no man might **BUY or SELL**, save he that had the **MARK**, or the **NAME of the BEAST**, or the **NUMBER OF HIS NAME**. Here is wisdom. Let him that hath understanding count the **NUMBER OF THE BEAST**: for it is the **NUMBER OF A MAN; and his NUMBER is SIX HUNDRED THREESCORE and SIX**.*"

"And I saw THREE UNCLEAN SPIRITS like frogs come out of the mouth of the DRAGON, and out of the mouth of the BEAST, and out of the mouth of the FALSE PROPHET.

"For they are the SPIRITS OF DEVILS, working MIRACLES, which go forth unto the KINGS of the earth and of the WHOLE WORLD, TO GATHER them to the BATTLE of that GREAT DAY OF GOD ALMIGHTY.

"And he GATHERED them together into a place called in the Hebrew tongue ARMAGEDDON.

"And the GREAT CITY was divided into THREE PARTS, and the cities of the nations fell: and GREAT BABYLON came in remembrance before GOD, to give unto her the cup of the wine of the fierceness of his wrath."

Revelation 16:13, 14, 16, 19

Taken from *The 21st-Century Revelation Seminar Teacher's Manual*, William Josiah Sutton

The **JESUS** of the Judeo-Christian Bible warned that there would be put in place laws that, if obeyed, will cause the Bible-believing Christian to deny **GOD** and His Christ. There are three things, however, that most pastors and Bible-believing Christians, most of the time, get confused about. Reader, the **MARK OF THE BEAST** is not **666**. If the reader will look closer at Revelation 13:17, he will soon discover that there are **three different warnings** that we had better not be identified with when the probation of mankind has ended. They are the **MARK, NAME,** and **NUMBER OF THE BEAST**, which is **666**. A diligent study of the **MARK, NAME,** and **NUMBER** of the **BEAST** are fully examined in the books, *Beware It's Coming - The Antichrist 666* and also in *Ancient Prophecies About The Dragon, The Beast, and The False Prophet.*

As pointed out in *Beware It's Coming - The Antichrist 666*, both the number of doom, "**666**," and also the symbol of the **Seven-headed Dragon** in the *BOOK OF REVELATION* can, indeed, be traced to the Chaldean religion of Astrology. Not only is the **MAN** who shall become the head of this coming **World Federation** to be **BRANDED** with this number, but the number **666, this number of doom**, is to also be involved in a **UNIVERSAL MARKETING SYSTEM**, as well, as Revelation 13:17 clearly states. This illustration to your right showing the proposed new money system that will eventually replace the world's currencies was taken from *The 21st-Century Revelation Seminar Teacher's Manual*, which this writer has been working on for five years now. This Teacher's Manual is full of **ILLUSTRATIONS** and diagrams which will guide its owner to give a 22-**SESSION STUDY** on the prophecies from the books of *Daniel* and *The Revelation.*

The reader will have in his possession overwhelming documented evidence to show on the screen how it is, indeed, this Masonic-based New World Order scheme which is presently globalizing the whole world. This is being orchestrated through international secret societies from both Masonic and Papal connections. The leaders of Freemasonry, the Pope, and American Protestant leaders are all involved in this through **Interfaith organizations**, like the Temple of Understanding Movement of the United Nations, who are connected with the Rockefeller Interchurch Center; the Riverside Church; the

The Economist
TAKESHITA COMES TO TOWN pages 17
DEMOCRATS IN DISARRAY page
AFGHAN EXIT pages 13 and
INVESTMENT BANKS PULL BACK page
PHOENIX PUBLIC LIBRARY
Get ready for a world currency
JAN 12 1988
TEN PHOENIX
10
2018

Cathedral of Saint John the Divine; and the Wainwright House, where the United Nations was first hatched by John D. Rockefeller, Jr. and his sons and their business associates back in 1941.[21]

About 600 years before **JESUS** walked this earth among mankind, the prophet Daniel pointed out to King Nebuchadnezzar of ancient Babylon, which is now in the country called Iraq, that the people of Spiritualism (**PAGANISM**) would raise up **KINGDOMS** down through the centuries which would take the world by force from Daniel's day to ours. The first was Babylon, which Nebuchadnezzar ruled over. The next was the pagan Persian Empire, then the pagan Grecian Empire, and then followed Pagan and Papal Rome. There came other efforts to control most of the known world after them, but they never took the world under its domain as did Babylon, Persia, Greece, Pagan Rome, and Papal Rome.

Soon to follow was Papal Rome's biggest rival. **Muhammad** and his successors certainly used force to conquer the whole world; however, they never completely did and neither will they ever. **Genghis Khan**, whose name means "*universal ruler*," certainly tried. His death and destruction spread even further than what Alexander the Great had done. However, Genghis Khan's universal rule never took root, and the nations that he conquered recovered. Napoleon also sought to conquer the world, and so did the human devil called Hitler. However, Bible-believing Christians living in the 21st Century are seeing right before their very eyes how the world is, indeed, being globalized into another World Federation similar to that which the great rebel Nimrod at the Tower of Babel brought about against God in his day.

In the book, *Ancient Prophecies About The Dragon, The Beast, and The False Prophet*, I show with plenty of documented evidence how it was the **Rockefeller Family** and their associates at the secret society called the **Council on Foreign Relations** in New York City who were behind the establishment of the **United Nations**. The greatest prophet of this **New Age** and **New World Order** conspiracy during the 20th Century was **John D. Rockefeller, Jr.** who died in 1960. I show in this book with plenty of evidence how **John D., Jr**. did more to promote this Masonic-based New World Order conspiracy than anyone before him, other than, of course, the **House of Rothschild** in the Old World.

All this is old news to many Bible-believing Christians who have been following the progress of this New World Order scheme for 30 or 40 years or more. However, now militant ***ISLAM*** has stepped in to stop it. Muslim scholars think that this **NWO** is the **ANTICHRIST SYSTEM** which was foretold to come in both the **BIBLE** and the KORAN; and all the violence coming from the **Muslim Brotherhood** and its branches, like the Al-Qaeda, Hammas, and Islamic Jihad, is over the founding of modern-day Israel by **Edmond Rothschild** beginning in the late 1800s. Muslim secret agents and intellectuals are very aware of the **Rothschild** and **Rockefeller** connection with **Freemasonry** and its offshoot, the **Illuminati**, and their **Knights Templars'** forefathers. Please keep in mind that the **Muslims** fought against the **Merovingian Knights** during the **Crusades**. It was the Frankish Knight Charles Martel of the Carolinian period who earlier, at the Battle of Tours in A.D. 732, stopped Islam from spreading into the heart of Europe.[22]

In Book II of *In Gog They Trust?*, the reader will see firsthand the reason why **Muslims of the 21st Century** are violently against the **NWO** and the establishment of **modern-day ISRAEL** and why they mistakenly believe that this **NWO** scheme is being run by modern descendants of the **Khazar Jews** who are supposedly behind the **Zionist Movement**. Book II of *In Gog they Trust?* also shows with plenty of Muslim sources that the Muslim clerics' belief today about the **Khazar Jews** is the **ROOT** of the new Muslim uprising and is the cause of most of the terrible carnage that is going on today in Palestine and Iraq and the rest of the world.[23]

In the book, *Ancient Prophecies About Mysticism, Hollywood, and The Music Industry*, this writer was warning his readers about **Osama bin Laden** and his Muslim fanatics and the imminent threat of Islamic attacks on America two years before the destruction they caused on **9/11/2001**. It is very important that Bible-believing people become aware of how the books of *Daniel* and *The Revelation* foretold not only this **NEW WORLD ORDER** scheme of the **FREEMASONS**, but also its greatest rival, the **MUSLIM MILITANTS**, who are mainly from the Wahabbi division of Islam.

Although it is receiving terrible reports on the Nightly News because of the terror and carnage that some of its more fanatical disciples are causing now in the 21st Century, nevertheless, the truth is ***ISLAM*** is the fastest-growing religion in the world! The reason why Christian pastors are losing so many of their members to *ISLAM* is because they are presently not being taught in their seminaries about just what the claims of *ISLAM* actually are; hence, **pastors are not properly trained on how to deal with *ISLAM* on a spiritual level**.

Like it or not, today **Americans** are unwittingly being caught up in a dangerous conflict between the masterminds behind the International Order of **FREEMASONRY**, which has been secretly promoting this **NEW WORLD ORDER** since **1776**, and these **MUSLIM FANATICS**, who are violently against the Masonic ***NOVUS ORDO SECLORUM*** a.k.a. **NEW WORLD ORDER** scheme. As pointed out in my books, the origin of both the New Age and the New World Order schemes traces back in history to the **Bavarian Order of the Illuminati**. Gurus of modern-day Spiritualism have been secretly working to bring about a One-World Government with a One-World Religion, a One-World Monetary System, and a One-World Rest Day for nearly 230 years. There is overwhelming evidence today which proves that the founders of the secret society of the **Bavarian Illuminati** united their Order with **Freemasonry** in the year **1777**[24] and planned to use the Masonic **LODGES** as their vehicle to bring about their **New World Order scheme**.

Nevertheless, little did these conspirators of Europe and the United States know that the **GOD** of Abraham, whom they were/are secretly struggling to overthrow, foretold in the books of *Daniel* and *The Revelation* what this coming **WORLD FEDERATION** would be allowed to accomplish before He brings it to nothing. However, for now, let's turn our focus to the **NEW WORLD ORDER'S** biggest rival, who are the **MUSLIM TERRORISTS** today who are violently against it.

It is very important for Bible-believing Christians to understand that the SHAYKHS and MULLAHS of ISLAM are also tying in the NWO conspiracy with the prophecies from the Bible and their Koran. What *ISLAM* teaches about the ANTICHRIST is all based in what the *Qur'an* (*KORAN*) and their books found in the *HADITH* also warned about the people who make up **GOG** and **MAGOG**. The Muslims have among them their Doctors of Divinity and scholars and intellectuals, as Christians do. It was amazing to me when I first learned that Muslim scholars believe and teach similar views on the prophecies about the ANTICHRIST as Protestant Christian scholars do. However, Muslims call the **ANTICHRIST** - "***DAJJAL,***"[25] and Muhammad left them a confusing prophecy about the ANTICHRIST that, unless they turn from it, they will find themselves on the side of the ANTICHRIST.

However, my Bible-believing, Christian reader, **MUSLIMS ARE NOT ANTI-JESUS**; on the contrary, **JESUS** is at the center of their "Time of the End" prophecies, as well. Muslims believe that it will be **JESUS** who will personally destroy the **ANTICHRIST**. I was absolutely surprised years ago to discover how much Muslims love **JESUS**; however, like the Roman Catholics, the Muslim people, because of their rejection of the Judeo-Christian Bible, have been misguided in their beliefs about who **JESUS** really is and have received a false interpretation of just who **CHRIST** was, is, and is to come. As we shall see from their own words, the JESUS of the *KORAN* (Isa) is very different from that of the Biblical **JESUS** (IĒSOUS), and so is this also true about the Muslim interpretation of whom the **ANTICHRIST** is, as well.

The word "***ANTICHRIST***" means "***instead of***" and/or "***in place of***" and, reader, it is important to keep in mind today that the first "**ANTICHRIST**" was **SATAN** who tried to overthrow **CHRIST** in Heaven. The first human "**ANTICHRIST**" on earth after the Flood who tried to overthrow **GOD** on planet Earth was **NIMROD**, (See Genesis, Chapters 10 and 11) who built the first cities in what now is called **Iraq** and **Iran** which, along with the **State of Israel**, are the **hot spots** that are causing the most international trouble in the world today.

I have found by studying from their own writings that Muslim clerics argue over these important prophecies about the **ANTICHRIST** as do Christian pastors. I personally witnessed how **BIBLE PROPHECY** turns the honest-hearted Muslim back to the Biblical **JESUS**. There are Muslims, who don't want to hurt anybody and who are not depending on their **MULLAHS** to teach them about God, who can be reached. This may have been a surprise to the Christian reader when he or she just learned that there are Muslim clerics who are also presently warning their people about the prophecies which surround the **ANTICHRIST** from the Judeo-Christian Bible. Muslim clerics are also correctly pointing out to their followers that the prophecies which surround the **ANTICHRIST** are two-fold. Muslim scholars are showing that the **ANTICHRIST** is both a **SYSTEM** and a **PERSON**. Muslim clerics are also correctly warning their followers that before the **ANTICHRIST** makes his debut in **OUR AGE**, he will first inspire the **RULING CLASSES** of this present world to set up a **WORLD FEDERATION (NWO) against GOD.**[26]

Some Muslim clerics and scholars are also correct in warning their followers that this coming ANTICHRIST SYSTEM will be controlling the political and financial institutions of the nations of the world just before the arrival of the ANTICHRIST (See Revelation 13:16, 17) and that there is no other power on earth today which is doing just that than these wealthy financial and political leaders, who are members of the **International Order of Freemasonry**. Some Muslim clerics and scholars are also very aware that the RULING CLASSES of this world are high-ranking members of FREEMASONRY and their offshoots, and that it will be these Occult-based secret societies that will bring about this **NEW WORLD ORDER scheme** as predicted in the *BOOK OF REVELATION*.[27]

However, what most Muslim MULLAHS (priests) and scholars fail to mention is how there are and, will be, Bible-believing Christians who are also against this Masonic-based New World Order scheme and will never join with this **INTERFAITH MOVEMENT** of the **DRAGON** (SPIRITUALISM), the **BEAST** (PAPACY), and the **FALSE PROPHET** (APOSTATE PROTESTANTS) to form what **JESUS** called **BABYLON THE GREAT**. (See Revelation 16:13, 14; 17:5) Although **JESUS** does not call those who stay loyal to Him during these dangerous days by any church affiliation, He certainly points to those in the *BOOK OF REVELATION* who are really His **TRUE PEOPLE** and who this great **RED DRAGON** is after the most. In Revelation 12:17, we read:

> *"And the **DRAGON** was wroth with the woman, and went to make war with the remnant of her seed, which **KEEP THE COMMANDMENTS OF GOD**, and have the **TESTIMONY OF JESUS CHRIST**."*

As we shall see from their own words, Muslim clerics teach their followers that they will be fighting against all Christians, as well, in this **LAST GREAT BATTLE** called Armageddon because they are not aware of the Protestant Christians who are also opposed to Mr. Bush's plans to help bring about any New World Order.

In the meantime, I was surprised to discover how many thousands of Muslims were purchasing my books. One distributor told me that he just stood on the corner in New York City and within one month sold 2,000 copies of my books to **Black Muslims**. Later, one Muslim bookstore alone purchased 5,000 copies, and I couldn't figure out back then why Muslims were so interested in my books. At that time, I wasn't aware that Muslim clerics were also warning their brethren about this **NWO** scheme to globalize the whole world today. After learning the terms which Muslim extremists use to describe the **ANTICHRIST** and his system, I was able to tap in on their websites to see why they are so against Americans today and especially its **CIA**, which President John F. Kennedy wanted to abolish in America before he was murdered on November 22, 1963.

The Masonic-based **NWO** scheme was launched on **May Day, 1776**, and this Occult-based **World Revolution** was promoted in complete secrecy up until the mid-1960s when the **New Age Hippie Counter-cultural Movement** started to publicly and openly reveal what they were planning. Many of you, I am sure, remember the popular song of the 60s and 70s which was promoting the idea that "***THIS IS THE DAWNING OF THE AGE OF AQUARIUS***." However, the vast majority of worldly Christians, who loved this song but didn't catch what it was actually saying, still remained ignorant about the New Age Movement until Constance Cumbey, a Christian lawyer, in 1983 began to expose on Christian radio and TV programs what she wrote in her book, *The Hidden Dangers of the Rainbow*, about the **New Age Movement**. This was also the very year I began to expose the Illuminati, the New World Order, and the MARXIST REVOLUTIONS in my book, *The New Age Movement and The Illuminati 666*.

While Cumbey was pointing out in her book that the New Age was connected with Nazism, I took my readers back in time to the founding of the secret society of the Bavarian Illuminati. I showed how both the New Age and the New World Order Movements today derived out of the **Masonic Revolution**, which was launched on May Day, 1776. Loyal Americans, I showed back in **1983** with plenty of documented proof that both the **New Age Movement** and the **New World Order** are brothers and sisters and were born in the same stall of the **Bavarian Order of the Illuminati**.

When I first heard President **George Bush, Sr.**, who is a member of the Masonic-based **Order of Skull & Bones**, openly state that the first Gulf War with Saddam in Iraq was part of a **BIG IDEA** to bring about a **New World Order**, it was the first time I had ever heard any American politician talk openly about this Masonic scheme. Franklin D. Roosevelt, who was a **33° Freemason**, camouflaged it in his day as the **New Deal**. I knew of Bush Sr.'s former connection with the **CIA** and also of his connection with the **CFR** (Council on Foreign Relations), and I was almost undone when I heard these words come forth from his own mouth. Let's see what he said in his State of the Union Message in 1991:

> "*What is at stake is more than one small country; it is a big idea; a* ***NEW WORLD ORDER****, where diverse nations are drawn together in common cause* ***to achieve the UNIVERSAL ASPIRATIONS OF MANKIND*** *-- peace and security, freedom, and the rule of law. . . . the illumination of a thousand points of light. . .* ***The winds of change are with us now***."
>
> *Source: http://www.c-span.org*

Reader, the sure Word of Bible Prophecy shows us that there will never be **WORLD PEACE** until Satan and his **FALLEN ANGELS**, along with those whom he controlled, are finally destroyed in the **LAKE OF FIRE**. (See Revelation, Chapter 20) In 1 Thessalonians 5:3, the apostle Paul warned:

> "*For when they shall say, Peace and safety; then sudden destruction cometh upon them, as travail upon a woman with child; and they shall not escape*."

IN GOG THEY TRUST?

PART II

Those who have studied this **NWO** conspiracy for years should be aware that this ***Novus Ordo Seclorum*** started in America as an Occult-based World Revolution whose Masonic leaders cleverly hid this **NWO** Revolution within the American Revolution. This writer also shows with plenty of documented evidence in the book, *Ancient Prophecies About The Dragon, The Beast, and The False Prophet*, that Franklin, Jefferson, Paine, and Benjamin Rush were all apostles of this **NWO** scheme who did, indeed, promote this **Masonic Revolution within the American Revolution** and that, when the war with England was over, this Masonic-based **New World Order** scheme just simply continued up until this very day.

In the 18th Century, the Masons used the tyranny of the Roman Catholic Church as their springboard to launch their Masonic Revolution under the canopy of the **ENLIGHTENMENT MOVEMENT** a.k.a. **ILLUMINISM**. Now, the ruling class of Protestant America, most of whom are connected with **Freemasonry**, are using the war with Muslim militants as their vehicle to promote the New World Order scheme as former President Bush, Sr. clearly said in his State of the Union Message back on January 29, 1991.

My Muslim reader, in Part II of this study about the **Antichrist** and **Gog** and **Magog**, I will try my best to show you how Muslims, themselves, are unwittingly being conditioned to accept the **Antichrist** because of **Muhammad's** false interpretation of who the **Antichrist** really is. The original prophecies about the **Antichrist** (Dajjal) did not come from the *KORAN* or the books of the *HADITH*; they came from the Biblical **JESUS** through His apostles who wrote the New Testament. Reader, the **ANTICHRIST** is not a Jewish Messiah with bushy hair and crooked legs who shall be blind in **ONE EYE**.

The **ANTICHRIST** actually started His mission to overthrow **GOD in Heaven**. It is **SATAN** who is really "**THAT ANTICHRIST**" whom the apostle John warned about in 1 John 2:18. He warned that there would come "**MANY ANTICHRISTS**," not just one; but the last false christ will be **SATAN HIMSELF**. This invisible **FALLEN ANGEL** from the Bottomless Pit will openly manifest himself before mankind and pretend to be **JESUS** and will even appear as **JESUS** looks like now in Heaven.[28] In the meantime, this invisible Prime Minister of this world would, in these Last Days, have his own human agent, who would act as the visible head of his unseen KINGDOM, sitting on his **SEAT** of power in this world until he himself comes to claim it. The apostle Paul warned about this in 2 Thessalonians 2:3, 4, 9:

> *"Let no man deceive you by any means: for that day shall not come, except there come a FALLING AWAY FIRST, and THAT MAN OF SIN BE REVEALED, THE SON OF PERDITION: Who opposeth and exalteth himself above all that is called God, or that is worshipped; so that he as GOD sitteth in the temple of God, shewing himself that he is GOD. . . . Even him, whose coming is AFTER THE WORKING OF SATAN with all power and signs and lying wonders."*

My Muslim reader, are you aware that the man who wrote this warning from **GOD** was also, at one time, a **1ST-CENTURY TERRORIST** against Christians and sought to have as many Christians killed as he possibly could? It is true. Paul's name was Saul before his conversion to Christianity, and he was a Pharisee of the strictest order. Paul can be compared to those **SHAYKHS** and **MULLAHS** who are leading the **WAHABBI MOVEMENT** within *ISLAM* today or the Catholic priests who were hunting down Protestants because they did not recognize the Pope of Rome as the Vicar of Christ. Saul (Paul) was determined that he was going to do his best to destroy Biblical Christianity until he, one day, was made aware that he was following a false religious spirit. Let's again look on the other side of this dangerous conflict that Bible-believing Christians are caught in between today. Let's see more closely what the **Muslim Revolutionaries** are teaching about this **MASONIC-BASED NWO**.

American citizens, who have not the slightest clue about what is really going on between the **international Order of Freemasonry** and **militant *ISLAM***, are now finding themselves, as in the days of Saul (Paul), as sought-after targets, however, this time by **Muslim fanatics** who are the Masons' biggest rival and who have their own plans to bring about a **Muslim NWO**. To try to understand why Muslim fanatics want to kill all Americans, I will use the words of Muslim leaders and scholars to prove my point. Again, we will see that all this terrible carnage which the **Muslim TERRORISTS** are presently causing in both the Old and New World is over what **Muhammad** supposedly said back in the 7th Century about the **ANTICHRIST** and **GOG** and **MAGOG** and how the **FREEMASONS** are, in modern **Muslim eyes**, fulfilling what their prophet said would happen.

Muhammad used the word "***DAJJAL***" to refer to the **ANTICHRIST**. Here is one of the things **Muhammad** supposedly said about the **ANTICHRIST**:

> *"I have explained **DAJJAL** to you, but I fear that you might not have understood. **DAJJAL** will be short, and his legs will be crooked. The hair on his head will be extremely twisted. . . . If you have any doubt regarding **DAJJAL**, remember that your Sustainer (ALLAH) is not **ONE EYED** . . . ."*[29]

As this badly-translated statement from the *HADITH* says, **Muhammad** supposedly told his early disciples that this coming "***DAJJAL***" (ANTICHRIST) will be a **MAN** who only has the use of **ONE EYE**. Which eye it is Muslims are still confused about because some have written it is the right eye, while others have written it is his left eye. Therefore, Muslims think that the **MASONS** are being led by the ***DAJJAL*** (Antichrist) because they use the **ONE EYE** (ALL-SEEING EYE) as the symbol of their power.[30]

On the front cover of my book, *The New Age Movement and The Illuminati 666*, I just happened to place this MASONIC SEAL showing the **ALL-SEEING EYE**, which can be seen on the back of the American one-dollar bill. After finding out what the Muslims believe about the **one-eyed Antichrist**, I finally realized why the MUSLIMS were buying so many of my books. This MASONIC SEAL with its **ALL-SEEING EYE** is what caught the eye of Muslims, and they are still one of the best purchasers of my books today.

While holding a series of lectures on the prophecies from the *BOOK OF REVELATION* in Portland, Oregon, I was met face to face with a former Black Muslim, who was not coming to me to take my life, but said to me, "It was because of the information in your books that I have now left the Black Muslims and have become a Christian." Shortly, afterwards, my wife and I met another Black Muslim who attended my meetings in Portland and requested a study which lasted several weeks and which resulted in his renouncement of Islam. In Part II of this study, I hope to show my Muslim, Catholic, Jewish, and Protestant readers at least a little glimpse of how we all can discover how this DEVIL has cleverly deceived the whole world!

Although the followers of *ISLAM* are confused over the prophecies about the **ANTICHRIST**, they do have sound reason to believe that it is the adepts of **FREEMASONRY**, who are the leading power in the **UNITED STATES** and also in **EUROPE**, that are busy trying to bring about this coming World Federation, which was foretold in Revelation, Chapters 17 and 18. However, my Muslim reader, this is **NOT A JEWISH CONSPIRACY**, as you have been told by your **SHAYKHS** and **MULLAHS**. This Masonic-based New World Order scheme is, and always has been, a **SECRET LUCIFERIAN** plot to overthrow the world. Here's some proof. To your right, there is another Masonic scholar and author of Freemasonry named **Albert Pike, 33**.° He became the head of the underground Illuminati Movement in his day after Grand Master Giuseppe Mazzini of Italy died in 1871. Albert Pike was Grand Commander of the Southern Jurisdiction of the Scottish Rite of Freemasonry in the United States. Most American Protestant Christians have never heard of him. Nevertheless, and ironically enough, a bronze 11-foot statue of Albert Pike is proudly standing on **FEDERAL** land in Washington, D.C. It is located at 3rd and D Street, NW, not far from the **NATION'S CAPITOL BUILDING**. Please read what Pike wrote to his fellow Masons of what the **Luciferians** would do to bring about this coming ***ORDO AB CHAO***, which means "***ORDER OUT OF CHAOS***," and ***NOVUS ORDO SECLORUM***, which means "***NEW ORDER OF THE AGES***" a.k.a. ***NWO***. From the very beginning, this Masonic-based Illuminati

GENERAL ALBERT PIKE, 33°
Sovereign Grand Commander of the Ancient and Accepted Scottish Rite of Freemasonry of the Southern Jurisdiction, U. S. A.

"To you, Sovereign Grand Instructors General, we say this, that you may repeat it to the brethren of the 32nd, 31st, 30th degrees: The Masonic religion should be, by all of us initiates of the high degrees, maintained in the purity of the Luciferian doctrine. If Lucifer were not God, would Adonay (the Christian god) whose deeds prove his cruelty, perfidy, and hatred of man, barbarism and repulsion for science, would Adonay and his priests calumniate him?

*"**YES, LUCIFER IS GOD, AND UNFORTUNATELY ADONAY IS ALSO GOD.** For the eternal law is that there is no light without shade, no beauty without ugliness, no white without black. For the absolute can only exist as two Gods: darkness being necessary to light to serve as its foil as the pedestal is necessary to the statue, and the brake to the locomotive . . . .*

"THE DOCTRINE OF SATANISM IS A HERESY; AND THE TRUE AND PURE PHILOSOPHIC RELIGION 'IS THE BELIEF IN LUCIFER,' THE EQUAL OF ADONAY; BUT LUCIFER, GOD OF LIGHT AND GOD OF GOOD, IS STRUGGLING FOR HUMANITY AGAINST ADONAY, THE GOD OF DARKNESS AND EVIL."

La Femme et L'enfant dans La Franc-Macconnerie Universelle, by A.C. De La Rive, p. 588;
Occult Theocrasy, Lady Queenborough, pp. 220, 221
Quoted from Fourth Reich of the Rich, Griffin, p. 70, 71

Movement, whose adepts have been Luciferians, has always been promoted under complete secrecy, and its members took (take) a **blood oath**, under the penalty of death, if any of them reveal(ed) any of their secret plans to overthrow the whole world. However, the Biblical **JESUS** said in Luke 8:17, 18:

> *"For nothing is **SECRET**, that shall not be made manifest; neither any thing **HID**, that shall not be known and come abroad. **TAKE HEED THEREFORE HOW YE HEAR**: for whosoever **HATH, TO HIM SHALL BE GIVEN**; and whosoever **HATH NOT**, from him **SHALL BE TAKEN** even that which he seemeth to have."*

In Hosea 4:6, it plainly states that **GOD'S PEOPLE ARE DESTROYED for LACK OF KNOWLEDGE** and, in 2 Thessalonians 2:10, 11, the Scriptures clearly warned, long before the **Papal, Islamic,** and **Masonic Revolutions** were launched, how those who have not **THE LOVE OF THE TRUTH** would **RECEIVE A STRONG DELUSION** and would **BELIEVE A LIE**. However, on the other hand, **JESUS** promises those who do have the **LOVE OF THE TRUTH**:

> ***"AND YE SHALL KNOW THE TRUTH, AND THE TRUTH SHALL MAKE YOU FREE."***
>
> ***John 8:32***

As pointed out, there are **THREE WORLD POWERS** which are presently globalizing the world into an unlawful World Federation. They are the adepts of the people of Spiritualism, the Papacy, and the American apostate Protestants who are slowly fusing themselves together today into a One-World Government with a One-World Religion, a One-World Monetary System, and a One-World Rest Day. All the people of the world who join this are unwittingly being corralled by **Luciferians** into their New World Order scheme that was first launched on **May Day, 1776**. It is not by chance that these Luciferians chose **MAY DAY** to launch their Occult-based World Revolution against Christ and His people. Among Luciferians and modern-day witches, May Day is called **BELTANE DAY**, which is the second most important **FESTIVAL** of the Druid **YEAR**. To the Wicca witches of the world today, it is when their god ***PAN*** of the **WINTER** and their goddess ***DIANA*** of the **SPRING** copulate and make things grow, which erring Christians today celebrate by dancing around the Celtic **PHALLUS** symbol called the **May Pole**.[31]

We have seen how the word "***CONSPIRACY***" written in Greek adds to **1776**. Let's now look closer at these Masonic revolutionary mottos which are in Latin and what they actually mean and just who the Freemasons are really exalting on these two seals seen on the back of the American one-dollar bill. To be able to understand just who these Latin mottos are pointing to, again, we must have some knowledge about just who were the chief gods of Mythology among the early descendants of Noah. Shortly after the Flood, the first society of people to promote the religion of Astrology were the **Chaldeans**, **Sumerians**, and **Phoenicians**. It was these people before the year 2000 B.C. who absolutely refused to hear God's Word preached to them and tried their best to swap the worship of ***EL*** for the worship of ***IL*** or ***ILU***, whom the Chaldeans placed as the supreme god of all their gods and goddesses. This ancient knowledge will not only help us see who is really being represented in these MASONIC SEALS on the one-dollar bill, but also who this Arabian god **ALLAH** really is, as well.

Reader, as pointed out, I have been a student of ancient Archaeology and ancient Mythology since 1970 and, after I started my own investigation of **Freemasonry** and the **Illuminati in 1971**, I discovered by studying the doctrines of Freemasonry from their own Masonic publications and by comparing their doctrines with the religion of Astrology that **FREEMASONRY** is nothing less than **BAAL WORSHIP** revived. Freemasonry in America has clothed itself in a **CHRISTIAN MANTLE** to help draw **unsuspecting Christian men into their LODGES**. This writer expecially shows in Book II how Freemasonry infiltrated both Catholic and Protestant churches. On the next page, there is a list of the pagan gods and goddesses which was taken from my *21st-Century Revelation Seminar Teacher's Manual*. This list is only showing the main pagan gods and goddesses whom the ancient Chaldeans, Sumerians, and Phoenicians worshipped in their heyday.

THE CHALDEANS USED THE NAME *ADUNNA-IRTSITI* TO DESCRIBE ALL OF THEIR GODS THE SUMERIANS CALLED THEIR GODS THE *ANUNNAKI*

	CHALDEAN	SUMERIAN	PHOENICIAN
Sky-God	Ilu	An (Anu)	IL
Earth Goddess	Ningal	Ki (Nintu)	Astarte
Sun-God	Beltus (Shamash)	Utu (Nikkal)	Baal-Shamesh
Moon-God	Sin (Nanna)	Nanna (Sin)	Yarikh (Sin)
Wind, Air & Storms	Enlil (Ningirsu) Zu, Anzu	Enlil	Baal-Hadad
Fire	Nusku	Gibil	Al Ait
Water	Oannes (god of sea) god of science & wisdom	Enki (EA) (fresh waters) Apsu	Dagon (also of grains) Asherat (goddess)
Sea	Bau (goddess of sea)	Tiamat (goddess of sea)	Baalat (goddess of sea)
Underworld	Nergal	Nergal Ereshkigal (goddess)	Melqart (Hercules)
Science, Crafts & Magic	Hermes (Oannes) Nabu, Nebo	EA (Enki)	Kothar
Goddess of Love & War	Rhea	Inanna (Ishtar)	Anat
Messiah-god	Tammuz	Dumuzi	Adonis
God of Plagues	Edem (Erra)	Nergal	Resheph (Resef)

TAKEN FROM *IN GOG THEY TRUST?*, BOOK II, WILLIAM JOSIAH SUTTON

There have been hundreds of them which were later adopted by the Egyptians, Persians, Greeks, and Romans. In this diagram to your left, I only placed just their most popular gods and goddesses. I am sure that there may have been a few others, but these shall be sufficient enough. Both the Bible and ancient History show that both the ancient **ISRAELITES** and the ancient **ISHMAELITES** were also fooled by the clergy of their day into worshipping and sacrificing to these same false gods.

The apostle Paul pointed out that these false gods that our ancient ancestors were fooled into worshipping were actually "**DEVILS**" who were **PRETENDING TO BE GODS**. Let's read what the apostle of **JESUS CHRIST** said in 1 Corinthians 10:20, 21:

> *"But I say, that the things which the* ***GENTILES*** *sacrifice, they sacrifice to* ***DEVILS, AND NOT TO GOD****: and I would not that ye should have fellowship with* ***DEVILS****. Ye cannot drink the* ***CUP OF THE LORD****, and the* ***CUP OF DEVILS****: ye cannot be partakers of the Lord's table, and of the table of* ***DEVILS****."*

In other words, the **mixing of paganism** with the **worship of GOD** is absolutely forbidden. However, this writer shows through all of his volumes overwhelming proof of how this very thing has been repeated by not only the ancient **Jews** and the **Ishmaelites**, but also by the Roman Catholics, Muslims, Freemasons, and the American Protestants, as well! Reader, Baal Worship is as active today as it was in the days of the ancient Israelites. There has come a **FALLING AWAY** from Biblical Christianity by mainstream Christians. This illustration on the next page was taken from *The 21st-Century Revelation Seminar Teacher's Manual* and shows the ancient Israelite clergy commanding the Jews to worship the Sun-god toward the East. In Chaldean Astrology, the incarnation of the Sun-god was **TAMMUZ** whom the Phoenicians of Canaan worshipped as ***ADONIS***, who was born at the **Winter Solstice** (December 21 or 25), and who, in the myth, died in the FALL but resurrected during the **Spring Equinox** in March (Easter). The ancient **Ishmaelites** living in **Petra** worshipped **Tammuz** as ***DUSHARES*** to whom the **Nabataeans** erected a huge Temple in his honor.[32]

*"He said also unto me, Turn thee yet again, and thou shalt see greater **ABOMINATIONS** that they do.*

*"Then he brought me to the door of the gate of the **LORD'S HOUSE** which was toward the north; and, behold, there sat **WOMEN WEEPING FOR TAMMUZ**.*

*"Then said he unto me, Hast thou seen this, O son of man? turn thee yet again, and thou shalt see **GREATER ABOMINATIONS** than these.*

*"And he brought me into the inner court of the **LORD'S HOUSE**, and, behold, at the door of the temple of the Lord, between the porch and the altar, were about **FIVE** and **TWENTY MEN**, with their **BACKS TOWARD THE TEMPLE OF THE LORD**, and their **FACES TOWARD THE EAST**; and they **WORSHIPPED THE SUN TOWARD THE EAST**."*

Ezekiel 8:13-16

TAKEN FROM *THE 21ST-CENTURY REVELATION SEMINAR TEACHER'S MANUAL*, WILLIAM JOSIAH SUTTON

Notice here that the Israelite women are said to be weeping for **TAMMUZ** and that they worshipped the Sun toward the East. Do not mainstream Christians observe the same pagan custom borrowed from Baal worshippers during their **Sunrise Services on Easter SUNS-DAY**? Above all the gods was the **KING** of the gods, who was the bright Sky-god ***ILU*** to the Chaldeans, ***ANU*** to the Sumerians, and ***IL*** to the Phoenicians, but to ***EL*** or ***ELOHIM*** of the Judeo-Christian Bible this ancient **Sky-god** is nothing less than that **OLD SERPENT**, the **DEVIL**, and **SATAN, WHICH DECEIVETH THE WHOLE WORLD**. (See Revelation 12:9)

Grand Commander **Albert Pike** pointed out in his book, *Morals and Dogma*, of which this writer has a copy, that **LUCIFER** used the various gods and goddesses of the religion of Astrology to camouflage himself before mankind. However, as we shall read from his own words, **Pike** urged that only the higher ranks of Freemasonry were to be made aware that the god of the Masons is not **ADONAI**, but **LUCIFER**. It is a historical fact that the Russian witch **Helena P. Blavatsky**, 33°, who co-founded the Theosophical Society in 1875 in New York, was one of the few women who ever became a 33° Freemason. **Blavatsky**, like Pike, was a Luciferian, as well, and so was her successor, **Annie Besant, 33°**, and **Aleister Crowley,** 33°, the founder of the secret society of the **O.T.O.** (American branch) and the father of the **HEAVY METAL** and **PUNK ROCK MUSIC MOVEMENT**. Crowley was also a 33° Freemason, and so was **Alice Ann Bailey,** who worked so hard to establish the **United Nations** and who was also an open and avowed worshipper of **Lucifer**. These people are some of the most honored heros of the New Age Movement today.

Is my Christian reader a member of **Blue Lodge Freemasonry**? Have you really understood what you are involved in? Let's read why from the pen of Grand Commander and **Luciferian, Albert Pike, 33°,:**

> *"The BLUE DEGREES are but the outer or portico of the Temple. Part of the symbols are displayed there to the INITIATE, but he is INTENTIONALLY MISLED BY FALSE INTREPRETATIONS. IT IS NOT INTENDED THAT HE SHALL UNDERSTAND THEM."*[33]

ORIGIN OF THE LATIN MOTTOS, *ANNUIT COEPTIS* AND *E PLURIBUS UNUM*

ANNUIT COEPTIS
means
"He has approved our beginnings"

The origin of the Latin motto, ANNUIT COEPTIS, can be traced to the pagan Roman poet named VIRGIL. Virgil was a worshipper of the ROMAN SKY-GOD JUPITER whom the Greeks earlier worshipped as ZEUS. The Phoenicians worshipped their Sky-god as IL, and the Chaldeans called him ILU, whom the Sumerians worshipped as ANU. The Latin motto, ANNUIT COEPTIS, was originally taken from part of the phrase that Virgil had written for the worship of Jupiter.

E PLURIBUS UNUM
means
"One out of many"

Taken from *The 21st-Century Revelation Seminar Teacher's Manual*, William Josiah Sutton

My Christian reader, it was none other than Grand Master of Freemasonry, **Benjamin Franklin**, and **Thomas Jefferson** who originally designed this Masonic Seal which is seen on the back of the one-dollar bill. This Masonic Seal was adopted by American politicians who were Masons themselves and who were running the United States government. This Masonic Seal with its revolutionary slogan, "***NOVUS ORDO SECLORUM***," which means "***NEW ORDER OF THE AGES***" and in astrological terms means the ***Age of Aquarius***, was not seen on the back of the American dollar bill until after the **Federal Reserve Act** was passed in the year 1913. By the way, the **Federal Reserve** is not a government-run bank. This Masonic Revolutionary Seal was placed there in **1933** by the New Age Socialist **Henry Wallace** who was later forced out of office as Vice President of the United States because of his ties with modern-day Spiritualism and Marxism (Socialism). Let's again see from the *Occult Illustrated Dictionary* by Harvey Day, Kay & Ward, Oxford University Press, NY, 1976, pp. 56, 57, just what these Latin mottos mean which are seen in these two seals:

> *"The emblem shown is an Egyptian pyramid in the apex of which appears the* ***THIRD EYE OF CLAIRVOYANCE. ANNUIT COEPTIS****, the inscription under the upper circumference, means* ***'HE PROSPERS OUR UNDERTAKING,'*** *and that in the lower,* ***NOVUS ORDO SECLORUM****, means* ***'NEW ORDER OF THE AGES,'*** *referring to the Gold, Silver, Bronze, and Iron Ages which comprise 26,000 years.* ***THE AQUARIAN AGE*** *in* **astrological terms**. . ."

This illustration to your left was also taken from *The 21st-Century Revelation Seminar Teacher's Manual*. The *Occult Illustrated Dictionary* didn't mention what the ***E PLURIBUS UNUM*** (in Latin) means. According to *Webster's New Dictionary of the English Language,* page 630, "***E PLURIBUS UNUM***" means "***ONE OF OUT MANY***" which these **18th-Century Masons** hoped to accomplish in the Latter Days. As pointed out, first the **Freemasons in England** planned to unite the **13 colonies** into a **United States** and then, later, they planned to unite the world into a universal **Masonic republic** based on **Plato's Dream** about establishing a **New Atlantis**.[34]

The New Age prophetess Helena P. Blavatsky's main theme in her books was the establishment of a **New Atlantis**, which in Greek Mythology was destroyed by ZEUS, the Sky-god, for the misuse of the advanced technology that was given to the **Atlanteans**. As the previous illustration shows, the Latin slogan, *Annuit Coeptis*, is exalting Jupiter, the Roman Sky-god, not the **GOD** of Abraham. The word "***BABYLON***" means "***CONFUSION***;" in Bible prophecy, it symbolizes **SPIRITUAL CONFUSION**, and here is another perfect example.

As the United States has their Intelligence-gathering operatives working within the National Security Agency and the CIA, so do these Muslim fanatics, who are deadly rivals of Freemasonry, have their own. The worst of them are those who are connected with the **Muslim Brotherhood** that was founded in Egypt back in **1928**. This secret society of Muslim **terrorists** is a 20th-Century offshoot of the secret society of the **Assassins** of 11th-Century Persia who founded their brand of *ISLAM* in **1090**. This was the very year that the **Merovingian Knight** named **Godfroi de Bouillon** founded the secret society of the **Priory of Zion** in Jerusalem. It was from the **Priory of Zion** that the Gnostic Order of the **Knights Templars** sprung later in **1118**, and this is also where the secret society of the Freemasons have their roots.[35]

This mysterious alliance between the **Muslim Assassins** and the **Knights Templars** is examined more in Book II of *In Gog They Trust?* I show from both Muslim and historical sources how the **TEMPLARS** formed a secret alliance with the "**ASSASSINS**" in an effort to overthrow the **Abbasid Dynasty of Baghdad** who, at this time, was the ruling class of *ISLAM* during the Arab Dispensation.[36]

The **ASSASSINS** were the **Osama bin Ladins** of their day; however, all of their Muslim revolutionary efforts were aimed at the **Sunni Muslims** in an attempt to destroy **ORTHODOX ISLAM** instead of the Christians. Like the secret society of the **Priory of Zion** in Jerusalem, the secret society of the **ASSASSINS** from Persia, from which our English word "***ASSASSINATE***" derived, was a conglomeration of the various branches of **SPIRITUALISM** which were blended with the teachings of Orthodox Sunni Islam, which, by the way, has denounced the **ASSASSINS** as heretics and also sought to route them out of *ISLAM*.

The illustration on the next page was taken from *Ancient Prophecies About Mysticism, Hollywood, and The Music Industry*. It is showing an **American Shriner Mason** today wearing his **Muslim FEZ**. The truth about Freemasonry and its origins should help those **Protestant Christians** who have entangled themselves with these **Masonic LODGES** to seek to get themselves untangled! This writer shows from Muslim publications that the **Knights Templars** (Freemasons) borrowed many of their crafts from **Sufi Illuminism** as this photograph of an American Shriner clearly shows. Since the early 1970s, this writer has also been studying the prophecies about **Muhammad** and the **Arab** and **Turkish Dispensations** of *ISLAM* as predicted in Revelation, Chapter 9. Like this writer did with **Freemasonry** and the **Illuminati**, I launched my own investigation into the origin of *ISLAM*, as well.

Muslim clerics today claim that *ISLAM* is not a new religion, but just an extension of the Judeo-Christian faith and that the **GOD** of the Hebrews and Christians is the same god of *ISLAM*. However, I prove in the books, *Ancient Prophecies About Mysticism, Hollywood, and The Music Industry* and Book II of *In Gog They Trust?*, that nothing could be further from the truth about this. This independent reseacher shows that the **GOD** of the Judeo-Christian Bible and the god of the *KORAN* are not the same God by using the *KORAN* and the books from the *HADITH,* ancient History, and Chaldean, Sumerian, and Phoenician Mythology.

The truth is this Arabian god named **ALLAH** was the supreme pagan god of the northern Arabians centuries before the time of **Muhammad**. At one time, he was the head of the pantheon of gods and goddesses at the Kaaba in Mecca until his worship gave way to the Nabataean Moon-god Hubal. Like the Chaldeans, Sumerians, and Phoenicians of Babylonia, the northern Arabians, who lived across the Persian Gulf from ancient Babylonia, adopted their gods but gave them Arabic names. The truth is the sacred SHRINE in Mecca (the Kaaba) housed a total of **360 different gods** and **goddesses** from different pagan beliefs as various merchants from different parts of the Old World traveled through Mecca and traded their merchandise.[37]

The city of **Mecca** where Muhammad grew up and founded *ISLAM* was an ancient center of WORLD TRADE and an OASIS from the desert sands. Today, the city of Mecca is both the religious and

The above picture shows a Shriner proudly wearing his Islamic red "fez" of the Order of the Mystic Shrine of Freemasonry. According to the Encyclopedia of Secret Societies & Fraternal Orders, Axelrod, pages 224 and 225, the Shriners were originally set up by 13 Master Masons in 1871 in NYC as a drinking club. The true name of this elite branch of Masonry is the Imperial Council of the Ancient Arabic Order of Nobles of the Mystic Shrine. The Shriners certainly show the origin of Freemasonry in their ORDER. Their LODGE is known as a TEMPLE, and some of the ornaments of their TEMPLES include both the Bible and the Koran and a foot-square Black Stone after the Black Stone in the Kaaba at Mecca. Shriners claim that their rituals and ceremonies date back to the son-in-law of Muhammad, the Caliph Ali. However, today, most Masons are unaware of just where the FEZ originated and why their ORDER of the 33° is centered in Islamic Mysticism. The name "FEZ" is the name of the city of Morocco where the blood of thousands of Catholic Christians flowed in its streets when the invading Arab Muslim armies swarmed out of Arabia into Morocco and Egypt like waves of locusts destroying those who would not worship Allah and accept Muhammad as his messenger. The conquering Muslims dipped their caps into the blood of their conquered Catholic foes as an expression of praise and thanks to their God Allah for giving them the victory. Many Shriners are completely ignorant about where their FEZ originated and spend as much as $1000 decorating them with gold and tiger claws. They are, however, an offense to the Orthodox Muslims.

cultural center of the Muslim WORLD. To prove my point, let's read the footnote written by a Muslim cleric on the Introduction page of the *KORAN* and what he admits about this Arabian desert-god **ALLAH**.

> *"Long before* ***Muhammad's call, ARABIAN PAGANISM*** *was showing signs of decay. At the* ***KA'BAH*** *the Meccans worshipped not only* ***ALLAH****, the supreme Semitic God, but also* ***A NUMBER OF FEMALE DEITIES*** *whom they* ***REGARDED AS THE DAUGHTERS OF ALLAH****. Among these were* ***AL-LAT, AL-'UZZA****, and* ***MANAT****, who represented the* ***SUN, VENUS,*** *and* ***FORTUNE*** *respectively."*
>
> *The Koran with Parallel Arabic Text, translated by Dawood, page ix, Penguin Books, London/NY, 1995*

Both ancient and modern mankind have often **confused** these two deities, ***El*** and ***IL*** (***ILAH***), as the being the same **GOD**. Let's take the word "***BABEL***." This name means "***GATE OF GOD***," but the Chaldeans originally spelled it "***BAB-IL***," which means "***GATE OF IL***."[38] This god to whom the pagan Chaldeans were referring was not the Hebrew **GOD** ***EL***, but ***ILU*** or ***IL*** who was the Sky-god to the Phoenician merchants. In Canaanite Mythology, ***IL***, the Sky-god, was the father of the Philistine god **DAGON** whose graven image kept falling on its face when the **Philistines** put the stolen Ark of the Covenant in the House of Dagon. (See 1 Samuel 5:1-12)

To begin to discover that **ALLAH'S** name also derived from this pagan word for god, which is ***ILAH***, all is needed is to go to a good dictionary and simply look at the origin of the word "***ALLAH***." You will quickly learn from a good dictionary that the name **ALLAH** derived from the old pagan Chaldean and Sumerian generic word for god, which is "***ILAH***."[39] The name ***ILAH*** was also a name these pagans used to identify with their Moon-god ***SIN***.[40]

The **Sumerians**, like the **Chaldeans** from whom they borrowed, absolutely refused to hear the Word of God (EL) spoken to them by Shem, the son of Noah, or later from the Hebrew Patriarch Abraham. Even though the **Sumerians** were from the same stock of people from which the Hebrews derived, they rejected the **GOD** of Noah, Shem, and Abraham all down through their history. The **Sumerian** international merchants, artisans, and magicians tried their best to blot out the name of the **HEBREW GOD** from under Heaven. The **Sumerian** word "***ILAH***," which derived out of the name ***IL*** or ***ILU***, simply means "*god.*" However, they believed that their ***ANU*** was god, and all the other gods and goddesses were just emanations of the one god ***ANU***. This pantheistic belief is still found among the Hindus and the Buddhists from whom the advocates of today's New Age Movement have borrowed many of their doctrines, as well. The **bright Sky-god** of the people of **India** is known as "***INDRA***," whom **Gautama Buddha** claimed to have been reincarnated as 36 times.[41]

Centuries before the birth of **Muhammad** in A.D. 570, the Arabian merchants of Mecca mingled themselves with the pagan Phoenician merchants who passed through Mecca as they traded their goods. Mecca was an ancient, major center of commerce before **Muhammad** received his new revelation about **ALLAH** and *ISLAM* in A.D. 610. The truth is, up until this time, **Muhammad** was also a pagan Arab merchant and a worshipper of the pagan gods and goddesses of his ancient ancestors who borrowed them from the Phoenician and Sumerian merchants. The name "***ALLAH***" is a **contraction**, which means it is two words that were combined to make one word. The Arabic word "***AL***" means "***THE***" and "***ILAH***" means "***GOD***;" hence, "***AL-ILAH***" means "***THE GOD***." The ancient pagan Arabians simply dropped the letter (I) in ***ILAH*** and connected it with the Arabic word "***AL***" that produced the name ***ALLAH*** which, by the way, also means "***THE GOD***" today. Muslims chant "***LA ILAHA ILL ALLAH MUHAMMADUR RASOOL ALLAH***" which means: "There is no god only Allah; Muhammad is the messenger of Allah."[42]

Like it or not, the truth is the Muslim god **ALLAH** was a pagan **GOD** of the Arabians centuries before Muhammad was born. This is a historical fact and even the most learned Muslim clerics cannot deny it today. At one time, **ALLAH** was the supreme god of **360 pagan gods**[43] and goddesses of the **Arabian pantheon** at the SHRINE in Mecca and, about **400 years** before the time of Muhammad, Allah lost his exalted position as their supreme god. **ALLAH** was bumped out of the position as being the supreme god of the Kaaba by the Arabian worshippers of the **Moon-god** named **HUBAL**.[44] It is here, however, that many Christian theologians, scholars, and pastors, who have some knowledge about the development of *ISLAM*, make a **huge error**. **ALLAH** was not the **Moon-god** of the pagan Arabians, as Christian theologians often try to teach in their writings. In northern Arabian Mythology, the **Moon-god Hubal** was originally just an emanation of **ALLAH**. There were no idols of ALLAH at the KAABA; however, among the **360 idols** of the Arabs, there were also sculptured figures of the infant JESUS and the Virgin Mary.[45] Muslim clerics use this false claim by Christians about **Allah** to show other Muslims how ignorant Christian scholars are. Koran 41:37 forbids the worship of the sun and moon.

Reader, **although ALLAH** was not the **Moon-god** at the Muslim SHRINE in Mecca, nevertheless, *ISLAM* is closely connected with pagan signs and symbols that come directly from Moon worship. Take a look at the symbol of *ISLAM* itself. Is it not symbolized by a CRESCENT MOON? Is not this ancient, pagan Sumerian sign of the Moon-god ***SIN*** proudly standing on top of Muslim MOSQUES found all over the world? It was the **NABATAEANS** who exalted **HUBAL** over **ALLAH** as the supreme god of the pagan Arabians in the northern part of Arabia. However, in the south, the pagan Arabians made "***ATHTAR***" their supreme deity. The truth is all **Muhammad** did in his heyday is this. Legends say that the founder of *ISLAM* and Ali, his brother-in law, pulled down from the roof of the Kaaba the graven image of **HUBAL**, the **Moon-god**, and made it into a step to enter the **Kaaba**. He went on to cleanse the **SHRINE at Mecca** of all its **360** idols of its **gods** and **goddesses**. However, he continued the pagan worship of **ALLAH**. Muhammad simply claimed that there is no god, but **ALLAH**, and he was his prophet.

As we will clearly see, there are some more facts from the ***KORAN*** itself that will show us that this god ***AL-ILAH*** (ALLAH), which is in Arabic and means "***THE GOD***," who rejects **JESUS** as the Son of God is not the same **GOD *(ELOHIM)*** of the Judeo-Christian Bible. Nevertheless, one of the ways Muslim clerics try to prove that **ALLAH** and the Judeo-Christian God are the same god is found in this doctrine of the ***Night Journey of Muhammad***, which can be found in 17:1 of the *KORAN*. My Muslim reader, this is another belief in *ISLAM* that I personally discovered to be a complete fallacy while studying the *KORAN* to see if ***ALLAH*** is the **Judeo-Christian God** or not. Again, I take no joy in exposing to you this **absolute fallacy of**

Muhammad's which I am about to show you. I just hope you and your family make your way through all this dangerous, as well as religious, confusion between the Jews, Christians, and Muslims and find the real **JESUS** of the Bible as I did.

The **SCIENCE** of Archaeology has made it easy for us living in the 21st Century to prove the origin of these false gods and goddesses of ancient Astrology, which Lucifer (the Dragon) and his evil angels pretended to be. In the book, *Beware It's Coming - The Antichrist 666*, there is plenty of archaeological, historical, and Biblical evidence that this religion of Astrology, that the Chaldeans symbolized as a **RED, SEVEN-HEADED, SERPENT-LIKE DRAGON**, was first based in the legends of **King Nimrod**, whom the Sumerians later called Gilgamesh, and his Queen **Sammu-ramat**, whom the Greeks called Semiramis.

As the diagram in this book shows, the pagan Chaldeans, Sumerians, and Phoenicians, before the year 2000 B.C., had their supreme god, as well, who was believed to have been their creator from whom they descended. Muhammad's false claim that ***EL*** or ***ELOHIM*** is also this ancient, pagan Arabian god (AL-ILAH) of the Kaaba is Muhammad's **#1 FALSE DOCTRINE**. The Islamic doctrine of the ***Night Journey and the Ascension of Muhammad*** from Jerusalem ranks **#2**. It is within this doctrine of *ISLAM* that Muhammad brought forth his bait to lure non-Muslim believers toward the idea that ALLAH is also the Judeo-Christian **GOD** which some, who call themselves PASTORS today, have swallowed hook, line, and sinker.

To your right, there is a Turkish painting showing Muhammad riding the ***Al-Buraq*** and the quote from 17:1 of the *KORAN* and also a quote from a well-known Muslim scholar about this important event in *ISLAM*. This supernatural creature that had the body of a white horse with wings and a woman's head called the ***AL-Buraq*** is said to have carried Muhammad from Mecca to Jerusalem and then to Heaven and back again all in one day. Muhammad's claim to have been carried from the ***KAABA*** in Mecca on the back of ***Al-Buraq*** to the site of Solomon's Temple in Jerusalem (*Laylat Al-lsra wa Al-Miraj*, which literally means "*the night journey and ascension*") actually lies at the heart of *ISLAM* , as well as Muhammad's claim to be the ***SEAL OF THE HOLY PROPHETS OF GOD***.

Surah (Chapter) 17:1 of the Koran states the following: "*Limitless in his glory is he who transported his servant by night from the Inviolable House of Worship (at Mecca) to the Remote House of Worship (at Jerusalem) - the environs of which we had blessed -- so that we might show him some of our symbols: for, verily, he alone is all-hearing, all-seeing.*"

Muhammad Asad's Commentary of Surah 17:1 of the Koran:

" *'The Inviolable House of Worship' (Al-Masjid Al Haraam) is one of the designations in the Qur'an to the Temple of the Ka'bah, the prototype of which owed its origin to Abraham (see Surah 2) and was the 'First Temple set up for mankind' (Surah 3, aya't 96), i.e., the first ever built for the worship of One god.*

" *'The Remote [lit., 'Farthest'] House of Worship,' on the other hand, denotes the ancient Temple of Solomon -- or, rather, its site -- which symbolizes here the long line of Hebrew prophets who preceded the advent of Muhammad and are alluded to by the phrase 'the environs of which we had blessed.'* "

Source: http://www.geocities.com/alummah2000/NightJourney.html

For nearly **1400 years**, Muslims have celebrated Muhammad's ***Night Journey*** from Mecca to Jerusalem as one of their founding doctrines in *ISLAM*. However, as we shall see, even Muslim scholars are admitting today that Muhammad's **Night Journey** could not have possibly happened at the site of Solomon's Temple in Jerusalem in A.D. 620, as their clerics claimed, and that it is, indeed, a grievous error in *ISLAM*. Nevertheless, history shows that this **Night Journey doctrine** of *ISLAM* has been the leading cause of untold millions of Jews, Christians, and Muslims, themselves, going down into untimely graves.

One of the first things this writer realized right away that helped him discover this great error in *ISLAM* was the date that this **NIGHT JOURNEY** of Muhammad's was to have taken place. Any Jew or Christian who has a good handle on Biblical history will also discover the same thing when he or she actually studies *ISLAM'S Laylat Al-Isra wa Al-Miraq*, which means "**NIGHT JOURNEY** and **ASCENSION**." This great Muslim event was said by well-known Muslim clerics, since the founding of *ISLAM*, to have taken place in the year **A.D. 620**, which was ten years after Muhammad received his **new revelation** about the *KORAN* and its religion of *ISLAM* in **A.D. 610**. This **Night Journey** doctrine, nonetheless, is the **backbone** to all of *ISLAM'S* claims to have the right to occupy and control the **city of JERUSALEM.**

Since **A.D. 638**, Muslims have fought bloody wars, starting with the Byzantine Christians and Papal armies, over what they think is their right to occupy and control the Holy Land. For nearly **1400 years**, the Muslim people have been told by their clerics that on the night of the 27th of their month of Rajab, Muhammad came to Jerusalem's **TEMPLE** (the Farthest Mosque) and ascended from a **ROCK** to Heaven to meet and receive instructions from his god **ALLAH**. However, the Temple Mount is only the **THIRD** most holiest site among Muslims. The **Kaaba** and the **city of Medina** are the first and second.

To your right, it shows the whole Muslim occupation of the Temple Mount area where they built the **DOME OF THE ROCK**, which covers the area from where ALLAH said in the *KORAN* Muhammad ascended to Heaven in **A.D. 620**. Please read the quotes about this from well-known Muslim writers that I placed there. My Muslim reader, **Solomon's Temple** was not there in **A.D. 620**. Muhammad could have not possibly entered into Solomon's Temple,

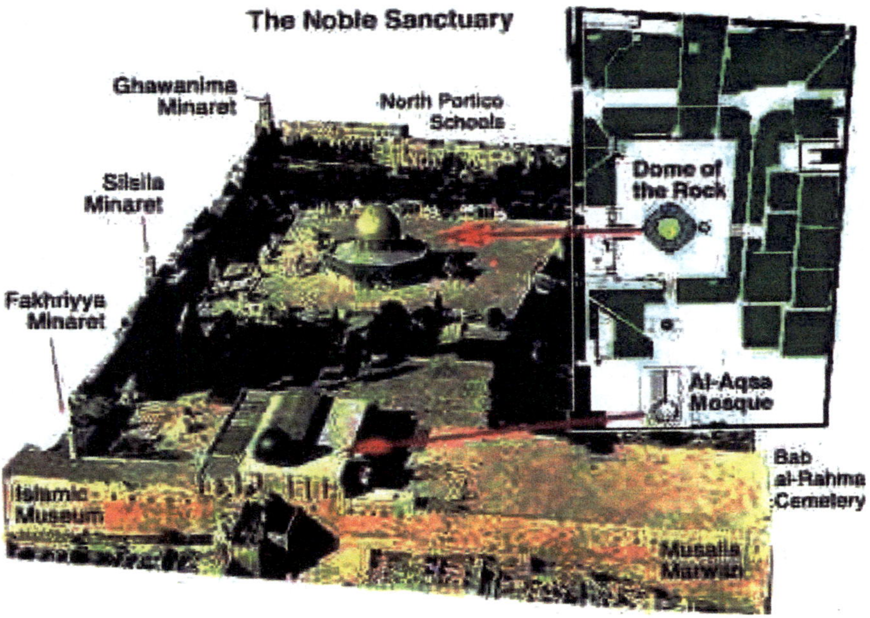

There are two sacred Muslim buildings that were built in the heart of Jerusalem where Solomon's Temple once stood. The Palestinian Muslims' living in the 21st Century deepest fears are that the Jews and the Christians will some day blow up the DOME OF THE ROCK to make way for a new TEMPLE. The DOME OF THE ROCK was built in A.D. 691 under the direction of Abd al-Malik ibn Marwan. The DOME OF THE ROCK, seen here in the upper center, is not a MOSQUE, but a MUSLIM SHRINE in honor of their prophet. Muslims actually have worship in a MOSQUE across from the SHRINE, seen at the bottom. It is known as the AL-AQSA MOSQUE which seats 5000. History records that the Arab Muslims took Jerusalem by force in A.D. 638 because they believed that their prophet in A.D. 620 was carried by night on the back of a supernatural being called Al-Buraq from the Kaaba in Mecca to the site of Solomon's Temple. (See Koran 17:1) Muslim clerics, for over 1300 years, have taught that when Muhammad entered the Jewish Temple in Jerusalem, he was greeted by a host of angels and all the prophets of the Hebrews, who were just standing in rows to greet and meet him. Then, the angel Gabriel supposedly asked Muhammad to lead them all in prayer and, afterwards, according to Muhammad, he ascended to the throne of ALLAH from a huge rock from the Temple Mount, which this DOME OF THE ROCK enshrines. Reader, this is another great, great falsehood taught by Islam's prophet. There was no Jewish Temple standing in Jerusalem in A.D. 620. It was completely destroyed in A.D. 70 by the Romans. In 620, the Byzantine Christians still had control of the Holy City and neither were there any Muslims nor Muslim MOSQUES in Jerusalem at this time in history.

as your clerics have taught, because the **Second Temple** was destroyed by the pagan Romans in **A.D. 70** as **JESUS** foretold in Matthew 24:1, 2. Let's see from a Muslim website why Muslims believe that *ISLAM* is just an extension of Christianity and that Muhammad was the last prophet to come after **JESUS**. This following quote is from the Noble Sanctuary Online Guide at ***http://www.noblesanctuary.com/HISTORY.html***:

> *"In the ninth year of the Prophet's mission, about 620 AD, Muhammad rose in the middle of the night to visit the Sacred Mosque in Makkah. After a time of worship he fell asleep near the Ka'aba. The angel Gabriel came to him and woke him from his slumber. He led the Prophet, peace and blessings be upon him, to the edge of the sacred Makkan mosque. Awaiting them was al-Buraq, a white winged beast 'whose each stride stretched as far as the eye could see.' Muhammad mounted al-Buraq and sped northwards with Gabriel to Al-Aqsa Mosque in Jerusalem, the Furthest Mosque.*
>
> *"When they reached Jerusalem the Prophet dismounted and prayed near the Rock. Abraham, Moses, Jesus and other prophets, peace be upon them all, gathered together to pray behind him. Muhammad was presented a vessel of wine and a vessel of milk. The Prophet chose the milk and Gabriel said, 'You have chosen the true religion.'*
>
> *"The Prophet then embarked on the ascension (**Miraj**) in which he, peace and blessings be upon him, received the command to pray five times a day and the revelation encapsulating the beliefs of Islam."*

Notice here that Muslims claim that "Abraham, Moses, Jesus, and other prophets" were said to have greeted Muhammad when he entered the Temple Mount area. This Muslim belief is trying to show Jews and Christians of the acceptance of Muhammad as a prophet by the great leaders of the Judeo-Christian faith by letting him lead them in prayer. However, it should be understood by Bible-believing Christians that, at this time, Abraham and the other prophets had been resting in their graves for centuries.

Somehow there has been a **great spiritual vail** placed over the eyes of Jews, Christians, and even Muslim clerics themselves by this **Prince of Darkness** who kept these grievous errors in *ISLAM* from being discovered sooner. After seeing this flaw in Islam myself, I turned to see if others have also discovered this today. Sure enough, even honest-hearted Muslims themselves are admitting to this great error in Islamic beliefs. Muslim clerics, who are now embarrassed by this fact that there was **no TEMPLE or Muslim MOSQUE standing in Jerusalem** in Muhammad's day, are now trying frantically to find some way to cover over this falsehood of their prophet. The reader can find on the Internet how the Muslim clergy are now desperately switching things around to make it appear that Muhammad wasn't referring to Solomon's Temple which he entered into and led the prophets of God in prayer. Some Muslim clerics are trying to prove that on the night that Muhammad journeyed into Jerusalem, he entered the **AL-AQSA** Mosque seen there at the bottom of the photograph. However, reader, the **AL-AQSA** Mosque was not there, either, in the year A.D. 620 when Muhammad's Night Journey from Jerusalem supposedly took place.

After realizing that their MOSQUE wasn't there either, Muslim clerics, who are not willing to admit to this grievous error in the *KORAN*, try to dismiss all of this by simply using the Arabic word "***MISJID***," which means "***MOSQUE***." They are trying to say that a MOSQUE doesn't mean just a building, but that it could also be considered to be just a "place of prostration" or worship, which could be done in the open air. Therefore, some Muslim clerics are now trying to claim that Muhammad prostrated himself in prayer before his god in the open air on the Temple Mount site. If this is true, then their prophet had to wade through the trash and dung to do it because the Byzantine Christians, who hated Jews, made the Temple Mount into their **trash dump** at this time. The truth is the Temple Mount area has laid in ruins since the Romans destroyed it. The last Islamic cover-up of this great delusion, that has caused bloody conflicts between the Arabs, Christians, and Jews, as well, even as I write, is that Muhammad didn't go to Heaven from Jerusalem, as originally thought by Muslims, but from Medina, the second most holy site in Islam. It is the city of Medina where Muhammad first established a **THEOCRACY**, and it was to be a model of what Muslims think the whole world will one day be.

SPECIAL DISPATCH

THE MIDDLE EAST MEDIA RESEARCH INSTITUTE

HOME | SUBJECTS | COUNTRIES | LANGUAGES | CARTOONS | SUBSCRIBE | ABOUT US | MEDIA | ARCHIVES

Archives

INQUIRY & ANALYSIS

SPECIAL DISPATCH

SPECIAL REPORT

SPECIAL ALERTS

NEWS TICKER HEADLINES

Go

SEARCH

Previous Page | E-Mail this document | Printer Friendly

Read this document in: Select a language:

MEMRI

THE MIDDLE EAST MEDIA RESEARCH INSTITUTE

Special Dispatch Series - No. 564

September 3, 2003 **No.564**

Egyptian Ministry of Culture Publication: The Prophet Muhammad's 'Night Journey' was Not to Jerusalem but to Medina

Ahmad Muhammad 'Arafa, *a columnist for* ***the Egyptian weekly Al-Qahira, which is published by the Egyptian Ministry of Culture****, wrote an article rejecting the established Islamic doctrine that the* ***Prophet Muhammad's celebrated "Night Journey"*** *(Koran 17:1) took him from Mecca to Jerusalem. 'Arafa, presenting a new analysis of the Koranic text, asserts that the Night Journey in Surat Al-Isra' (that is, "the Sura of the Night Journey") in the Koran does not refer to a miraculous journey from* ***Mecca to Jerusalem****, but to the Prophet's emigration (Hijra)* ***from Mecca to Medina****.*

It should be noted that the belief that Muhammad's Night Journey (Koran 17:1) was a miraculous journey to Jerusalem is one of the most important foundations of the sanctity of Jerusalem in Islam. There is an extensive body of Islamic traditions related to this belief, and these are explicitly or implicitly rejected by the author. This article constitutes a dramatic departure from a standard Islamic doctrine. The fact that this article was published in a government journal adds to its political significance. The following is a translation of the article, titled "Was the Prophet Muhammad's Night Journey to Palestine or Medina?" which was published on August 5, 2003: [1]

Where Is Al-Aqsa Mosque?

"'Praise be to Him who took His servant by night (*asra*) [2] from the Al-Haram [Sacred] Mosque [in Mecca] to the Al-Aqsa [literally 'the most distant'] Mosque, whose environs We did bless, so that We might show him some of Our signs, for He is the All-Hearing and All-Seeing One' (Surat Al-Isra'[17]:1).

"This text tells us that Allah took His Prophet from the Al-Haram Mosque [in Mecca] to the Al-Aqsa Mosque. Thus, two mosques are [referred to] here, the first of which is the Al-Haram Mosque, and the second of which is the Al-Aqsa Mosque. '*Al-Aqsa*' is a form of superlative which means 'the most distant.' Therefore, the place to which the Prophet was taken must be a mosque, and not a place where a mosque was to be established later, nor a place where a

When the Muslims conquered Jerusalem in **A.D. 638**, they found the **ancient Temple Mount** area of the Jews still abandoned and filled with all kinds of refuse. Did not your **Caliph Omar** (Umar), who conquered Jerusalem, order and force the Byzantine Christians in Jerusalem to clean up the **Temple Mount** area so he could build the first **Muslim MOSQUE** in Jerusalem for worship? Did he not build this **first Muslim MOSQUE** at the south wall of the **Temple Mount** so that the Muslim worshippers would be facing toward Mecca? Reader, again, **THERE WAS NO TEMPLE** or **Muslim MOSQUE** or the **Dome of the Rock** standing in **A.D. 620** in Jerusalem in Muhammad's day for him to have entered into or ascended to Heaven from. The Muslim occupation of the **Temple Mount** in Jerusalem didn't even begin until **A.D. 638**, which is some **18 years** after this **Night Journey** of Muhammad's was to have taken place.

Has the reader seen the recent dispatch from the Egyptian Ministry of Culture Publication dated September 3, 2003, to all their Muslim brethren worldwide? **The Middle East Media Research Institute** has now issued a statement from a respected Muslim newspaper columnist named Ahmad Muhammad 'Arafa from the Egyptian weekly *Al-Qahira* stating that Muhammad could not have entered into any **TEMPLE** or **MOSQUE** in Jerusalem, for 'Arafa and the Middle East Media Research Institute have also realized now that there was no **TEMPLE** or **MOSQUE** on the Temple Mount in Jerusalem in Muhammad's day for him to enter into. This dramatic departure from this Islamic doctrine about Muhammad ascending to Heaven from Jerusalem could stop the terrible carnage that Muslim **TERRORISTS** from the Muslim Brotherhood are causing today if they would simply realize this fact, as well. If the reader hasn't seen this dramatic statement from these concerned Muslim leaders, please log on to ***http://www.memri.org/bin/articles.cgi?page=archives&area=sd&d=sp56403***.

Another grand delusion that the people of *ISLAM* need to take a very close look at is Muhammad's interpretation of Bible prophecy which surrounds the predictions of the **ANTICHRIST** and the **ANTICHRIST System** which **SATAN** would use to bring about this coming World Federation that **JESUS** called **BABYLON THE GREAT**. This also needs to be readdressed by honest-hearted Muslims. My Muslim reader, the **ANTICHRIST** (DAJJAL) is not a white man with bushy hair and crooked legs or a blind-in-one-eyed human being with supernatural powers as Muhammad painted him. Although the **DEVIL** will always have a **MAN** who represents his invisible **KINGDOM** on earth, the truth is **SATAN himself** is predicted from the Judeo-Christian Bible to appear as **JESUS CHRIST** during the "Time of the End," which your Muslim clergy is completely in the DARK about. The very people that the **Shi'ites** of Iran point to as being the ***JUGE WA MA JUGE***, who are presently establishing the **ANTICHRIST (DAJJAL) SYSTEM**, back in the 12th Century secretly made an alliance with the Muslim *ASSASSINS* to overthrow the **SUNNI ABBASIDS** in Baghdad. This secret alliance between the **Muslim Assassins** and the **Knights Templars** occurred during the reign of King Baldwin II of Jerusalem. Did not the **KNIGHTS TEMPLARS** make the **Muslim DOME OF THE ROCK** their spiritual headquarters for 88 years? Did not the Knights Templars borrow much of their mystical knowledge from the Muslim SUFI SHAYKHS? Are they not called the **FREEMASONS** today?

The Shi'ite Muslims from Iran, who have called the people of America "**THE GREAT SATAN**," had better take a step back in time and take a good look at what their forefathers were up to when the Merovingian Knights ruled the Holy Lands from 1099-1187 and also just who this god **ALLAH** really is, for **JESUS**, who you claim will kill the **DAJJAL** (ANTICHRIST), also said in the *BOOK OF REVELATION* that this **OLD SERPENT**, the **DEVIL** and **SATAN**, **DECEIVETH THE WHOLE WORLD**. (See Revelation 12:9)

Both SUNNI and SHI'ITE Muslim clerics also mistakenly think that this whole **Masonic-based NEW WORLD ORDER** scheme is solely a **JEWISH** conspiracy to bring the whole world under their subordination. Muslim clerics, like the dangerous White Supremacist groups in America, think that it is only the **WALL STREET JEWS** (Zionists) who are controlling the events leading to the development of this Masonic-based **NEW WORLD ORDER**. As we will see shortly, Muslim clerics are also preaching to Muslims that all Protestant Christian churches in America are controlled by the **FREEMASONS**; and, therefore, the **Muslims** will have to fight another **Holy War** with the Christians, as well, because they think all the leaders of their churches are **FREEMASONS**. Learned Muslim clerics believe that the

FREEMASONS today are a counterfeit of *ISLAM* and stole much of their mystical knowledge and revolutionary plans from the Muslims during the time of the events that were occurring shortly before the **First Crusade** and then, afterwards, when the **Knights Templars** were the Royal Guards of the Temple Mount in Jerusalem.

After Godfroi de Bouillon and his Merovingian Knights slaughtered all the inhabitants in the city of JERUSALEM in 1099, about two decades later, the **Knights Templars** made the Muslim **Dome of the Rock** their own TEMPLE, and the **Al-Aqsa Mosque** located at the south wall of the Temple Mount became the Templars' MILITARY HEADQUARTERS until **Saladin** came in **1187** and won the Holy City back for the Muslims. During this time, Christian churches were converted to MOSQUES and the Muslim shrines were restored.

Except for a brief 16-year period between 1228-1244, Muslims controlled Jerusalem up until World War I when the British took control in **1917**. In the meantime, **Edmond Rothschild**, whose BANKING FAMILY has connections with the **Freemasons**, as well, in the late 1800s gave **14 million francs** for Russian and European Jews to buy up as much land in Palestine as they possibly could. The Rothschilds planned that the future headquarters of this **NWO** was to eventually be established in modern-day Israel. This is one of the reasons why learned Muslim clerics think that this **NWO** scheme is a Jewish conspiracy which is being run, behind the scenes, by the modern-day descendants of the **Khazar Jews**, who we shall take a look at shortly.

Muslim SHAYKHS, MULLAHS, and scholars of *ISLAM* today use the Internet to spread the **Gospel of Muhammad**, as we use the Internet to spread the **Gospel of Christ**. However, if a Bible-believing Christian is interested in winning a Muslim fanatic to the Biblical JESUS, he or she must not be a **cross worshipper** and/or a **pork eater**. If you are, Muslims will not trust anything you have to say if you ignore the Dietary Laws given by Moses. On the other hand, a Bible-believing Christian will learn that there are Muslims who really do not want to hurt anybody, and you can tap into the Muslim militant websites who do by simply knowing some of the Arabic terms they are presently using to bring about their plans and purposes. One word in particular that will open wide many green doors to see what these Muslim fanatics are planning to do to JEWS and CHRISTIANS is this word

"***DAJJAL***" and also the names "**GOG**" and "**MAGOG**." If the reader is interested in learning why Muslims are **hot against Americans**, just type in these words on your favorite search engines and see what you come up with. **You will see through Muslim eyes** what their grievances against America and Britain really are instead of trying to find it out by listening to **CFR**-controlled TV news broadcasts or by reading it from some bigoted Christian writer. Muslim militants refer to nominal Muslims, Jews, and Christians as "***MUNAFIQEEN***," which means "***HYPOCRITES***," and to those who refuse to believe ALLAH is GOD and Muhammad is his prophet as "***KUFFAAR***" (KUFR). Keeping this in mind, here is a quote from a Muslim militant organization's website ***http://allaahuakbar.net/free-masons/dajjal.htm***:

> *"The **DAJJAL-system**, is of course as we know is **FREEMASONRY**. Every single position in the **UNITED NATIONS**, the **EEC** and every position in the **BRITISH PARLIAMENT** is held by people who are **FREEMASONS**. Freemasonry has something in the region of 700,000 members in England and Wales, yet the British public hardly know anything about them.*
> *"About 60% of the Archbishops are **FREEMASONS** and secretly practice **DEVIL-WORSHIP** (see above mentioned books). If you want to know if a church is being used as a **MASONIC TEMPLE**, then look on the stained glass windows for a **MASONIC SYMBOL SUCH AS A 'SNAKE AND A DAGGER, OR A STAR OF DAVID.'***
> *"If the church is in the shape of a **GREEK TEMPLE**, then it is definitely used for **MASONIC PURPOSES**. In Liverpool, the* **Roman Catholic Cathedral** *has many pyramids, **MASONIC SYMBOLS. THERE MAY BE MUCH FEAR ABOUT DAJJAL, BUT THE FINAL VICTORY HAS BEEN PROMISED TO THE MUSLIMS. WHEREBY EVERY SINGLE JEW/FREEMASON SHALL BE PUT TO DEATH. THE WHOLE EARTH SHALL BE CLEANSED OF KUFFAAR ONCE AND FOR ALL**."* [SIC]

There are a number of Muslim websites, like this one, who are promoting hate propaganda against Jews and Christians in America and Europe today. However, this Muslim militant who wrote this also needs to become aware that many **Muslim men** also belong to the various **Orders of Freemasonry**, as do many **Christian men**, in the United States and England. Unfortunately, most of our **political leaders** in the United States and England today are members of **FREEMASONRY**, and Muslim terrorists are convinced that Masonic LODGES are secretly being run by modern **Khazar Jews**, instead of **Luciferians**.

Muslim clerics teach that Allah told Muhammad that a group of people would come ahead of the **Dajjal** (Antichrist) and prepare the world for him to take over and that a counterfeit society of JEWS, who do not follow the writings of Moses, would arise in the modern world and cause terrible destruction, chaos, and oppression on the Muslim people. Muslims refer to these counterfeit Jews as the **JUGE WA MA JUGE** (YAJUJ WA MA'JUJ).[46]

Another Muslim militant group who is using the Internet to spread their Gospel of Islam is known as ***MUSLIMSONLINE.COM***. They try to prove that the Jews who are running modern Israel today are descendants of the **ancient Scythians** (Magogites) of southern Russia. They point out that the **Khazar Jews**, whose descendants are running modern Israel today, are not from any of the 12 original tribes of the **Hebrew Jews**, but rather are directly related to the people of **GOG** and **MAGOG**. According to ***MUSLIMSONLINE.COM***, the names of **GOG** and **MAGOG** only appear in the *KORAN* in Chapter 18 and 21; and in Arabic, they are referred to as "***YAJUJ WA MA'JUJ***."[47]

In Book II of *In Gog They Trust?*, this independent researcher shows with overwhelming proof that all this terror and carnage that **Militant ISLAM** is spreading all over the world now in the 21st Century is, indeed, over the prophecies concerning who they think are representing **GOG** and **MAGOG**. We have already established with their own words that Muslim revolutionaries believe that the **DAJJAL** (ANTICHRIST) System is being established today by the **FREEMASONS of Europe** and **America**. I show in the above book with plenty of documented proof from Islamic sources that these 21st-Century militant Muslims believe that the founders of **Europe** and the **United States** were originally **descendants of MAGOG**, who was first to settle in Russia after the Flood. Hence, Muslim militants believe that the European and the American **RULING CLASSES** are **GOG** and **MAGOG** because they are their modern-day descendants who came from the sons of **JAPHETH**.

Muslims are taught by MULLAHS in the *KORAN* and the *HADITH* that the **ANTICHRIST SYSTEM** would first be set up and then the **ANTICHRIST** himself will first appear between **Syria** and **Iran**.[48] Muslims think that all the Jews and Christians will be fooled into joining with the **ANTICHRIST** because they rejected *ISLAM*. As a result, Muslims think that this whole **Masonic New World Order** today is an attempt to take over the whole world and make **JERUSALEM** the **CAPITAL** or **HEADQUARTERS** of their coming World Federation. We will see, however, that this prophecy from *ISLAM* is a mixture of both truth and error. However, the prophet Daniel and the apostle John did, indeed, write that the people who control the world in these Last Days will establish the **headquarters** of this coming **ANTICHRIST SYSTEM** in modern Israel. We will examine this shortly.

In the book, *The Real Truth About UFOs and The New World Order Connection*, there is a diligent study about the origin of the **ASHKENAZI JEWS** who make up at least 85% of the Jewish population today. The above book shows with plenty of documented proof that the **ASHKENAZI JEWS** are from **CELTIC** origin, not **HEBREW** (Semitic) origin, as Muslims are quick to point out from the Bible and history. Therefore, Muslim clerics argue that these White European Jews, who are running modern-day Israel in the 21st Century, are not the real chosen people to whom **GOD** originally gave the Holy Land for their **HOMELAND**.[49]

Muslim clerics also point out that the **JEWS** who established modern Israel in **1948** were mainly these Celtic Jews from Russia and eastern Europe whose ancestors were originally pagans, who established in southern Russia (Scythia) the **Khazarian Empire** in the 7th Century. Muslim clerics are also quick to point out from history that these **Celtic Jews**, who founded the **Khazarian Empire**, didn't become **JEWS** until after their **KING** named **Bulan** adopted Judaism from Jewish clerics who regularly traveled the Silk Road with Jewish merchants on their way to China.[50]

The reason why Muslim clerics have so much knowledge about the **Khazar Jews** is because it was these war-like peoples of what is now southern Russia who stopped the Muslim invaders from taking eastern Europe. It is interesting to note that while it was the Frankish Knight **Charles Martel** who stopped the Muslim invaders coming from Spain from completely taking over Europe, it was the **Khazar Jews** who stopped the Muslim invaders coming from the Caucasus Mountain region from entering into Europe.[51]

However, it also very eye-opening to discover that it is from this same Caucasus Mountain region that the Muslim prophecies about **GOG** and **MAGOG** begin. Let's read now what Muhammad supposedly dictated to his scribes to write in 18:93-99 of the *KORAN* about **GOG** and **MAGOG**:

> *"When he reached the valley between **TWO PALISADES**, he found people whose language was barely understandable. They said, O Zul-Qarnain, **GOG** and **MAGOG ARE CORRUPTORS OF THE EARTH**. Can we pay you to **CREATE A BARRIER BETWEEN US and THEM**? He said, My Lord has given me great bounties. If you cooperate with me, I will build a **DAM** between you and them. **BRING TO ME MASSES OF IRON**.*
> *"Once he filled the gap between the two palisades, he said, Blow. Once it was red hot, he said, Help me pour tar on top of it. Thus, they could not climb it, nor could they bore holes in it. He said, This is mercy from my Lord. When the prophecy of my Lord comes to pass, He will cause the **DAM TO CRUMBLE**. The prophecy of my Lord is truth. At that time, we will let them invade with one another, then the horn will be blown, and we will summon them all together."*

One very important factor that Bible-believing Christians must keep in mind is that the last book of the Judeo-Christian Bible, the *BOOK OF REVELATION*, was written in A.D. 95 or A.D. 96. The truth is the *KORAN* wasn't written until nearly 500 years later between A.D. 610 and A.D. 632. It actually wasn't in print until A.D. 650. Although there is no mention in the Judeo-Christian Bible of a **DAM** or **WALL** that was built between two palisades or two mountain peaks to shut the ancient **MAGOGITES** from coming out of their ancient HOMELAND shortly after the Flood, please keep in mind that this Muslim prophecy about **GOG** and **MAGOG** was not written around **2200 B.C.** when the giant descendants of **MAGOG** walked this earth. Muhammad didn't begin to dictate the verses in the *KORAN* until A.D. 610, which was over 600 years after the **BIRTH of Christ**.

The Judeo-Christian Bible, however, does refer to this area located to the extreme north of the Caucacus Mountains as "***THE LAND OF MAGOG***," as Ezekiel 38:2 plainly states. According to Josephus, the Greeks changed the Biblical name of the ancient "**MAGOGITES**" to "***SCYTHIANS***;" hence, the "***LAND OF MAGOG***" became known afterward as **SCYTHIA**. This **DAM** that was built to keep the **PEOPLE** of **GOG** and **MAGOG** out of the Middle East is shown in other translations of the ***KORAN*** to have been a **WALL** which was built of **IRON BRICKS** embedded in molten **COPPER**, rather than **IRON** and **TAR.**

Amazingly, the science of Archaeology shows that there was actually an ancient **WALL** built between two mountain peaks to seal up a mountain pass in the Caucasus Mountains in an effort to keep the ancient ***MAGOGITES*** from spreading into the Middle East. This ancient **WALL** was built at the southern end of the ancient city of **DERBENT** in what is known now as the most southern city in Russia. Ironically enough, this ancient **WALL** still has parts of it standing today, and anciently it was called by the local people - **GOG** and **MAGOG**. This **WALL** extended 50 miles, and it was made of bricks of iron and copper with huge iron gates and watchtowers. It was 29 feet tall and 10 feet thick, and its remains are located on the western shoreline of the Caspian Sea.[52]

The **Caucasus Mountains** extend some 750 miles between the Black Sea and the Caspian Sea, and they are impossible to cross except at its passes. The barbarian **MAGOGITES** start their history around **2200 B.C.** These barbaric people made their living by robbing and killing people in other countries around them. These **tribes of King Magog** were known **cannibals** and, after they robbed and killed their victims, they ritualistically feasted on the dead carcasses of their victims. Hence, this **WALL** of **GOG** and **MAGOG** was built across this 50-mile pass between the **Caucasus Mountains** and the Caspian Sea. It was, indeed, anciently built in an effort to keep these **barbaric people in Scythia** out of Mesopotamia. However, the *KORAN* teaches that this **WALL**, which separates **Scythia** and **eastern Europe from Asia**, was to be made low and the descendants of **Gog** and **Magog** would scatter throughout the world. Muslim clerics point out from Genesis 10:2 that **Magog** was a real person who was ancient Scythia's (Russia's) first king, who was a giant. Another militant Muslim group, who is trying to convince **non-Muslims** and **Muslims** that the **Europeans** and **Americans** are the modern-day **GOG** and **MAGOG** of the 21st Century, is based in London and call themselves the **ISLAMIC PARTY OF BRITAIN**. What they say about **GOG** and **MAGOG** can be examined by logging onto ***http://www.islamicparty.com/commonsense/14gog.htm***.

The **ISLAMIC PARTY OF BRITAIN** has an article on their website entitled "***IN GOG THEY TRUST***?" . To prove that England's Frankish descendants are part of the people who are the modern **GOG** and **MAGOG** today, these Muslim militants bring out some eye-opening facts about British history. They are quick to point out today how **GUILDHALL** in London has **TWO GIANT-STANDING IDOLS** whose names are **GOG** and **MAGOG** that, for the past 500 years, stood as guardian deities of the streets of London. Over the centuries, there have been made more than one set of these gods called **GOG** and **MAGOG**. The ancient, pagan British sacrificed human beings to them before Christianity arrived in the British Isles. Muslims point out how the **British MONARCHY** has a day set aside each year to parade their two idols through their streets as the guardian deities of London, which I might add, is, unfortunately, very true.[53]

Muslim clerics today try to bring credibility to the *KORAN* and its god ***AL-ILAH***, who actually traces to the Phoenician Sky-god ***IL*** (***ILAH***), by using the history of the **WALL** which separated the **SCYTHIANS** (Magogites) from spreading into the Middle East. Muslim clerics point out that the **WALL of GOG and MAGOG** was ordered to be built by their god ALLAH and that it did crumble as ALLAH had predicted in the *KORAN* 18:98. However, archaeologists point out that this ancient **WALL of GOG and MAGOG** in Derbent was built and destroyed and rebuilt several times down through the long centuries, and this was done long before the birth of *ISLAM* in A.D. 610. So the question is, "How could this Arabian god ***AL-ILAH*** (ALLAH) have prophesied in the *KORAN* about the fall of the **WALL OF GOG AND MAGOG**, as we read in the 18th Chapter of the *KORAN,* when this **WALL of GOG and MAGOG** was both built and toppled centuries before the *KORAN* was written?" Reader, the *KORAN* did not exist during 2200 B.C.-168 B.C. when all this was taking place.

Muslims, nonetheless, from a child up are programmed by their clerics to believe that the Judeo-Christian Bible has been corrupted by both Jewish and Catholic priests and that ***AL-ILAH*** gave them the *KORAN*, the inspired word of their god, to replace it. However, before the ***KORAN*** was written, we saw the warning that those who reject the **TRUTH** found in the Bible will end up believing in a "**STRONG DELUSION**" and because they received not the "**LOVE OF THE TRUTH**" that they might be saved, they will "**BELIEVE A LIE**." (See 2 Thessalonians 2:10, 11)

Nevertheless, in the *KORAN* 85:21, 22, it states that **it is without error** and that there is a **MASTER COPY** of the *KORAN* written on a tablet in Heaven. However, another very damaging fact to the credibility of the *KORAN* and the Muslim faith, on which it is based, is the *KORAN'S* history about **ABRAHAM**. Again, please keep in mind that Muhammad never learned to read or write, and he supposedly dictated the *KORAN* to his scribes between **A.D. 610-632** as they wrote it down. Muhammad died in **A.D. 632** and his scribes published the first complete copy of the *KORAN* in A.D. 650, some 18 years after the death of their prophet.

Besides the truth about **ALLAH** as originally being a pagan god of the Arabs centuries before the birth of Muhammad in A.D. 570 and that there was no standing **TEMPLE** in Jerusalem for its prophet to enter into during his "***NIGHT JOURNEY***" (*KORAN* 17:1) in **A.D. 620**, Muhammad's story about **Abraham** being delivered by the **FIRE of NIMROD**, which is found in 21:51-71; 29:16, 17; 37:97, 98 of the *KORAN,* is another proven fallacy that this mystic of *ISLAM* deceived the Arab people into believing.

There are two main sources that Muslims use to back up their beliefs. One is the ***KORAN***, of course, and the other are the books found written in the ***HADITH***. The following is a quote from a Muslim website at *http://www.geocities.com/minutesage1/stories.html* that used a story found in the ***HADITH*** to comment on these previous verses found in the *KORAN* about **ABRAHAM** and what the great rebel **NIMROD** and his followers tried to do to him.

> "***NIMROD*** *was the ruler who threw* ***PROPHET ABRAHAM*** *into the fire.* ***NIMROD'S daughter Raghda*** *was present at that incident. When she saw that the fire did not harm* ***ABRAHAM*** *and that he had escaped safe and sound from it, she asked him who had saved him?* ***ABRAHAM*** *replied that it was* ***ALLAH THE ALMIGHTY WHO SAVED HIM****.*"

Muhammad's scribe who wrote this tried to convince its reader that Abraham was a worshipper of ALLAH, as well.It should be noted here, again, that Muhammad could not read or write but, if he could have, the founder of the religion of *ISLAM* would have read from the writings of Moses in the Torah, which he claimed to accept, that **King NIMROD**, who built the Tower of Babel in **2230 B.C.**, lived about **234** years **BEFORE ABRAHAM WAS BORN**. According to Moses, Abraham wasn't born in **UR** of the Chaldeans until **1996 B.C.**[54] The truth is **ABRAHAM** simply did not live in the time of **NIMROD**.

However, let's see now how another very **serious error** found on the pages of the *KORAN* and the *HADITH* has made this world in the 21st Century a very dangerous place for **JEWS, CHRISTIANS,** and **MUSLIMS**, as well, to live in because of Muhammad's false interpretations of the prophecies found in the Judeo-Christian Bible about the **ANTICHRIST** and **GOG** and **MAGOG**. In the 21st Chapter of the *KORAN*, there is also another description of what was going to happen to this world after the **WALL OF GOG AND MAGOG** would be toppled and the **MAGOGITES** from the North were free to enter the Holy Lands, the Middle East, and the rest of the world. It is because of this **GRAND DELUSION** of Muhammad's found in 21:96, 97 of the *KORAN* that Muslim youth today are strapping bombs on their bodies to kill as many **AMERICANS** and **JEWS** as they can.

The **WALL OF GOG** and **MAGOG**, which is now laid waste just south of the 5,000-year-old city of Derbent in southern Russia, was, at one time, the boundary line between the ancient Scythians (Magogites) and the ancient Persians and later the Khazars Jews and Arabs. This toppling of the **WALL** of Gog and Magog, among Muslims, lies at the root of the very reason why **Osama bin Laden** planned a sneak attack on New York and Washington. To prove my point again, let's read from 21:96, 97 of the *KORAN* and see what ***ALLAH*** supposedly said through Muhammad about **GOG** and **MAGOG**:

> *"Not until **GOG** and **MAGOG REAPPEAR**, will they then return - they will come from every direction. **THAT IS WHEN THE INEVITABLE PROPHECY WILL COME TO PASS**, and the disbelievers will stare in horror. 'Woe to us; we have been oblivious. Indeed, we have been wicked.' "*

Reader, Muslim clerics **AIM** this Islamic prophecy about **GOG** and **MAGOG** from the *KORAN*, which was taken from **Ezekiel, Chapters 38** and **39**, directly at the **KHAZAR JEWS** who, around the year A.D. 650, established themselves as a multi-cultural society of people in southern Russia. Muslim extremists try to point out from **21:96** of the *KORAN* that the ancient peoples of **GOG** and **MAGOG** were to "**REAPPEAR**" in history again and that they began to reappear in the **JEWISH KINGDOM** of the **KHAZARS** in Scythia (Russia). Muslim clerics and scholars today erringly believe that the **KHAZARS** were descendants of **KING MAGOG** who first settled this land shortly after the Flood.

After conquering the nations of the area, the **KHAZARS'** domain stretched from the Black Sea to the Caspian Sea. After being proselytized by both Byzantine Christians and Muslim missionaries, they chose Judaism as a way of sidestepping from being dominated over by the Byzantine Christian kings or by the **CALIPHS** of ***Islam***.[55] During their 366 years, the **Khazars** went from being a pagan Sun-worshipping society of mixed peoples into a powerful, rich and advanced, Jewish civilization ruled by powerful Jewish **KINGS** whom the Arab Muslims, during their heyday, were never able to completely overthrow. However, a great deal of Khazarian wealth came from the sale of East European Slavs as slaves, outrageous taxes, and by usury. Muslim clerics know from history that it was a coalition of forces of Russian and Byzantine Christians in **A.D. 965-1016** who finally overthrew the **Khazars** and scattered them throughout the world.[56]

Muslim militants go on to teach that it is these modern descendants of the **KHAZARIAN JEWS** who are the modern **GOG** and **MAGOG** peoples whom they refer to as ***JUGE WA MA JUGE***. According to Muslim thinking, these modern descendants of the Khazars are also presently running **FREEMASONRY** and the **ZIONIST MOVEMENT**. Muslims urge that they are not the original **Hebrews** and that these **ZIONIST JEWS** who founded the **State of Israel** in 1948 have no direct bloodline to Abraham; therefore, they have no lawful nor rightful claim to the **Holy Lands** as their inheritance.

However, the **Arabs** also need to look at their own false claims to the **Holy Lands**, as well. Moses wrote in the Torah that **Holy Lands** were promised to Abraham's son ***ISAAC*** (See Genesis 17:19-21), not to ***ISHMAEL***. *ISLAM'S* claim that the **DOME OF THE ROCK** marks the spot on the Temple Mount where Muhammad ascended to Heaven during his Night Journey is as false as **NIMROD** trying to burn alive Abraham in fire.

My Muslim reader, what your Muslim clerics have written about the Khazar Jews is also based on a greatly distorted view of ancient History, as well. The **KHAZARIAN JEWS** do not trace to King "**MAGOG**," the son of **JAPHETH**, according to Moses, but to "**GOMER**," Magog's older brother and the father of **Ashkenaz** and **Togarmah.** (See Genesis 10:2) The Khazar Jews, my Muslim reader, were from a **MIXED RACE** of **Caucasian** and **Mongolian peoples** who became known in history as the **HUNS** and the **TARTARS** from whom **Attila the Hun** (A.D. 406-453) arose earlier. The Khazar Jews were of these same various branches of the Turks, not the Scythians.[57]

The **KHAZARS** were not from the same lineage as the **Ashkenazi Jews**. While the ***KHAZARS*** were a **MIXED RACE**,[58] the *ASHKENAZI*, on the other hand, remained purely **CAUCASIAN** (Celtic). The **KHAZAR JEWS**, whom your clerics refer to as the ***JUGE WA MA JUGE***, were actually just a branch from these same mixed-Turkish peoples who were originally from China and from whom the **OGHUZ** and the **SELJUK TURKISH TRIBES** also derived. If you need more convincing, just look at an ancient bust of a Khazarian warrior that archaeologists have discovered from a Kharzarian site. Although the **Khazars** were sometimes known for their blue eyes, reddish hair, and fair skin, their oriental eyes are clearly seen. You may view some archaeological discoveries of Khazarian Art by logging on to ***http://www.fortunecity.com/marina/cyprus/125/march/31/***.

Was not **OTHMAN**, who founded the Ottoman Empire in A.D. 1299, a **TURK** of a mixed race? Was he not also of a mixed race of Caucasians and Mongolians who were also of fair complexion, but with dark eyes and black hair? My Muslim reader, the **Khazar Jews** were not originally **Scythians** (Magogites), as your Muslim clerics and Christians have erringly taught. The truth is it is the Muslims from **IRAN** (Persians) whose ancient ancestors trace to the **Scythians**, not the **Khazars**.[59] The **Khazars** were originally from **Turkey**, not from **Russia**. The truth is the **Khazars** were run out of their **HOME-LAND of Turkey** by the invading Arab Muslims and sought refuge in southern Russia in the 7th Century.

The ancient people who first settled Anatolia (Turkey) were, indeed, originally **Caucasians** who derived from **GOMER'S** two sons named **Ashkenaz** and **Togarmah**. However, there developed from post-Flood times many various branches of the Caucasian race, as did those of the Semitic race. Many of the tribes that derived from **GOMER'S** two sons, who first founded what is now called Turkey, mingled themselves with the various branches of the Mongolian peoples. However, there was a tribe from the **House of Togarmah** that has remained purely **Caucasian**. They are known as the **White Huns** to which the **Ashkenazi** peoples, who were also forced out of Turkey by Muslims, can be traced. A branch of these **White, war-like Huns** also became known in history as the "**Hephthalites**," who worshipped the Iranian Fire-god ***Ahura Mazda*** of the Zoroastrians.[60] It was from the Persian prophet **Zoroaster** that **Jewish Mysticism** (Cabalism) derived. It is a well-known fact that at least 85% of the Jewish population today are made up of these **ASHKENAZI JEWS**.[61]

Muslim clerics are right in stating that the **ASHKENAZI JEWS** who founded modern Israel in **1948 are not from the direct BLOOD-LINE of Abraham** and, therefore, have no rightful claim to control the Holy Lands. The **ASHKENAZI** are, indeed, Celtic, not Semitic, Jews. Like the **Khazar Jews**, these **ASHKENAZI JEWS** earlier were pagans who later adopted **JUDAISM**. The truth is neither the **JEW** nor the **MUSLIM** has any right to control the Holy Lands.

The **Creator**, who owns this world, in **A.D. 34** gave an eviction notice to the **HEBREW JEWS** to leave the **Holy Lands** and never return for their rejection of **CHRIST** as their Messiah. **JESUS**, who was a **HEBREW JEW**, not a Muslim, told the rulers of the Hebrews of their day in Matthew 23:38: "***BEHOLD, YOUR HOUSE IS LEFT UNTO YOU DESOLATE***." Just 36 years later in **A.D. 70**, the pagan Romans came and utterly destroyed the **CITY** of Jerusalem, just as **JESUS** predicted in Luke 13:35 and Matthew 24:1, 2.

The Temple Mount laid in ruins until the Muslim revolutionaries invaded. As we saw, history shows that, 568 years later, Muslims invaded the Holy Lands and took Jerusalem **by force**, beginning in **A.D. 638**. Like the Ashkenazi Jews today, the Muslims, as well, do not have any spiritual or lawful right to control **ISRAEL** either. The beliefs connected with the **Dome of the Rock**, that covers the area where Solomon's Temple once stood, were built on a falsehood based on Muhammad's ***Night Journey*** doctrine, which even learned Muslims are beginning to realize never occurred in A.D. 620 at Jerusalem. In the meantime, Muslim terrorists, who remain in the **DARK** about these important issues of the day, continue to kill many **JEWS** and **AMERICANS** because of a false Muslim belief about their **NOBLE SANCTUARY** that they supposedly established on the Temple Mount back in the 7th Century.

What is so amazing to me today is how the Jews and mainstream Christians, **NWO** advocates, and **MUSLIM SHAYKHS**, who are all presently struggling to control the **Holy City**, are all completely in the **DARK** about what the angel Gabriel showed the prophet Daniel that the **GOD OF ABRAHAM** said will really happen in the **Holy Lands** in this **AGE** in which we live. Reader, it will be **SATAN, not GOD,** who will establish his **HEADQUARTERS** in the **HOLY LANDS**. This notion by **American PROTESTANT churches** of helping re-establish **ISRAEL AS A JEWISH STATE** has been **ONE GRAND DELUSION** which was not only foretold in Bible prophecy, but was inspired by Lucifer himself. As we shall see shortly, the angel Gabriel showed both the prophet Daniel in the Old Testament and the apostle John in the New Testament that it will be "**THAT ANTICHRIST**," who is **SATAN**, that will establish his **SEAT** of modern **BABYLON THE GREAT** in **ISRAEL**, not **JESUS CHRIST!** As pointed out, Revelation 16:13-19 clearly shows us that there were to be **THREE WORLD POWERS** symbolized as **THREE BEASTS** which would form **MODERN BABYLON** during the **Time of the End** in which we are surely living. These three world powers today are representing the **PEOPLE OF MODERN-DAY SPIRITUALISM**, the **PAPACY**, and the **AMERICAN APOSTATE PROTESTANTS** who are presently fusing together through **INTERFAITH ORGANIZATIONS**. This mixed multitude of **PAGAN, CATHOLIC,** and **PROTESTANT FAITHS** is, indeed, trying to establish modern-day **ISRAEL** as the **CAPITAL** of this coming, short-lived **World Federation**, just as Bible prophecy foretold!

These spiritually-confused people are busy trying to globalize the whole world into a **ONE-WORLD GOVERNMENT** with a **ONE-WORLD RELIGION**, a **ONE-WORLD MONETARY SYSTEM**, and a **ONE-WORLD REST DAY**. Those who refuse to connect themselves with this modern Tower of Babel Movement of the 21st Century will soon find themselves not able to **BUY** or **SELL**, save he that had the **MARK**, or the **NAME OF THE BEAST**, or the **NUMBER OF HIS NAME**. In the meantime, these spiritually-confused Muslim militants, who have their own Islamic Revolutionary plans for a **NWO**, are also promoting **WAHABBISM**; and all **secular MUSLIMS, JEWS, CHRISTIANS,** and **PAGANS** who reject their Muslim **REVIVAL** are to be killed. Let's now see how all this great spiritual confusion is shaping up things to bring about a "***TIME OF TROUBLE, SUCH AS NEVER WAS SINCE THERE WAS A NATION EVEN TO THAT SAME TIME***" as the angel Gabriel predicted to Daniel in Chapter 12:1.

The word "***KUFR***" is the word Muslim clerics use in a very derogatory way to describe those of us who reject *ISLAM*, its god **ALLAH**, and **Muhammad** as a prophet. As pointed out, the "***DAJJAL***" (Antichrist) was said by **Muhammad** to be a **WHITE MAN** who will be **BLIND IN ONE EYE** with **CROOKED LEGS** and **BUSHY HAIR** with the letters ***KFR*** written on his forehead. Followers of Muhammad will also find that this description of the **ANTICHRIST** by Muhammad and his successors is another false interpretation of Bible prophecy. However, what Muhammad said about the **ANTICHRIST SYSTEM** from the Judeo-Christian Bible is true. Muhammad pointed out to his followers that the ***DAJJAL***

(ANTICHRIST) ***SYSTEM*** must be established **FIRST** before the **PERSON**, who is the **ANTICHRIST**, appears to deceive the whole world. However, what the Islamic clerics have interpreted about **GOG** and **MAGOG** and the **BATTLE OF ARMAGEDDON** from Revelation 16:13-19; 20:7-10 is another **GREAT, STRONG DELUSION** which, if Muslims do not turn from it, they will surely find themselves on the side of the **ANTICHRIST**.

Like the Jews, Muslims are looking for a messiah to come and deliver them from their oppressors. Muslims teach that when the **FREEMASONS** establish this **ANTICHRIST SYSTEM**, which is coming to us as ***NOVUS ORDO SECLORUM***, then **ALLAH** will send a **MUSLIM MESSIAH**, whom they call "***IMAM MAHDI***," who will supposedly destroy this coming **DAJJAL SYSTEM**. Today, Muslim clerics think the **DAJJAL SYSTEM** is being established by the modern descendants of the **KHAZAR JEWS,** who are the hidden rulers behind **FREEMASONRY** and the **ZIONIST MOVEMENT**, which founded **MODERN ISRAEL** in 1948.

On the next page, there is a diagram showing where **JESUS** will, according to Muslim thinking, descend from Heaven and where he will kill the ***DAJJAL*** (**ANTICHRIST**). I found this diagram while searching the Muslim websites which are centered around the ***DAJJAL*** and **GOG** and **MAGOG**. According to *ISLAM*, after the MASONIC-BASED ***DAJJAL*** (ANTICHRIST) **SYSTEM** is destroyed by the Muslim ***IMAM MADHI***, then **JESUS** will descend from Heaven into the city of **DAMASCUS**. From Damascus, **JESUS** will make His way south where Muslims believe he will kill the **ANTICHRIST** (***DAJJAL***). However, reader, it is here where we can find how the Muslims are being conditioned, by the very one whom they claim to be against, to fall for **SATAN's** crowning deception.

The apostle Paul, whom Muslim clerics reject, clearly warned us how we can tell the difference between CHRIST and the ANTICHRIST. The Christian apostle warned us that **JESUS WILL NEVER SET FOOT ON PLANET EARTH AT HIS SECOND COMING**. The apostle Paul pointed out that when the Biblical **JESUS** comes to rescue His people, **WE SHALL SEE HIM COMING IN THE CLOUDS WITH POWER AND GREAT GLORY. OUR LORD WILL THEN CAUSE US TO MEET HIM IN THE AIR!** This is a very important

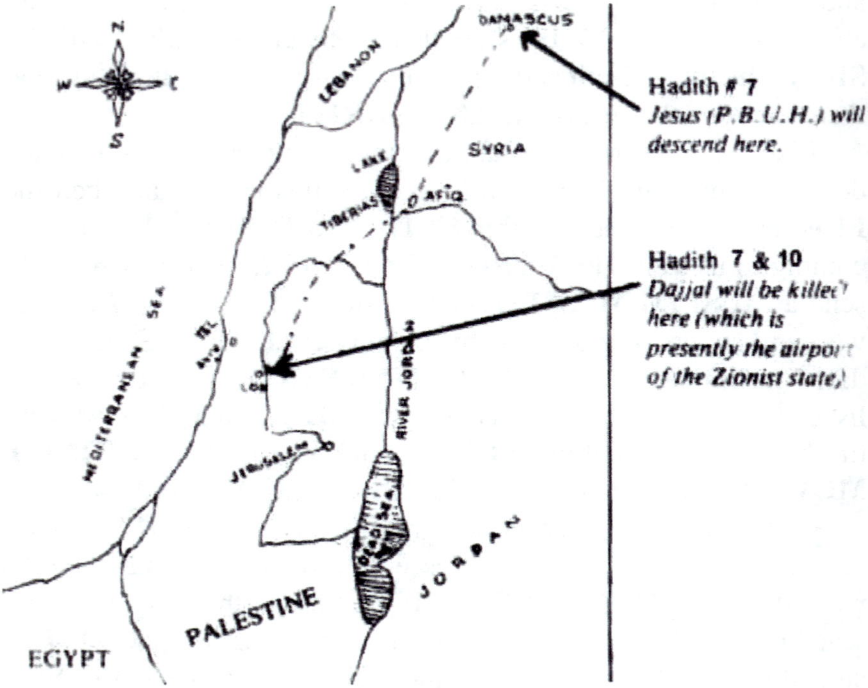

The Bible describes in a vivid language the corruption, destruction, and death typifying the end of times. We see the godly forces confronting the evil of Satan, the Antichrist, and Gog and Magog. We learn that the cataclysmic events will take place in the Middle East. But still the picture needs to be completed. Unanswered questions need to be answered. Who are Gog and Magog? Where will Jesus return? Where in the Middle East will Jesus confront the evil military forces? What nation(s) will supply the forces? Where will the Antichrist be slain?

The Holy Prophet Muhammad(p) has prophesied about several events that will occur just before the advent of the day of judgment. Among these, Muhammad(p) has foretold the return of Jesus(p), which will materialize when a one eyed claimant to divinity (Antichrist) will attempt to misguide the humanity into worshipping him. Messiah will descend from the heavens in Damascus, pray behind Imam Mahdi, pursue and kill the Antichrist, destroy the savage and unbelieving armies of Gog and Magog, and bring peace and brotherhood to the world. Christians will recognize the truth and accept him only as a Messenger of God, the religion of God (Islam) will justly rule the world.

Bible prophecy found in 1 Thessalonians 4:16, 17 which will also help us distinguish the difference between **CHRIST** and the **ANTICHRIST**. Long before the Papacy, Islam, and Freemasonry arose, **JESUS** warned us in Matthew 24:24 that there would come **false christs** and **false prophets**. However, the last **false christ** will be the **DEVIL** himself. **SATAN** will **personate JESUS CHRIST** and shall walk among men in these last closing days of Earth's history. He is "**THAT ANTICHRIST**" which the apostle John warned about. However, this prophecy below about **JESUS' SECOND COMING** will give the Bible-believing Christian understanding in how not to be fooled into following this last counterfeit christ.

> "*For the **LORD HIMSELF** shall descend from heaven with a **SHOUT**, with the voice of the **ARCHANGEL**, and with the **TRUMP OF GOD**: and the **DEAD IN CHRIST SHALL RISE FIRST**: Then we which are **ALIVE** and remain **SHALL BE CAUGHT UP TOGETHER WITH THEM IN THE CLOUDS, TO MEET THE LORD IN THE AIR**: and so shall we ever be with the Lord.*"
>
> *1 Thessalonians 4:16, 17*

As clearly pointed out, **JESUS** will not walk down from Damascus to hunt for the **ANTICHRIST** so that He can kill him. The Biblical **JESUS** is a different JESUS than that of the *KORAN*. The apostle Paul said we will **meet Him in the AIR**, not on earth, at this time. Even though Muslims often use the Judeo-Christian Bible when pointing out the **Antichrist**, they have misinterpreted and rejected what it teaches about Christ and the **Antichrist**. To see that this is true, please read these Muslim quotes to your left about what they interpret from the prophecies about the **Antichrist** (DAJJAL) and the manner in which **JESUS** will destroy him and the host of Gog and Magog that unite with him. Let's see some more of how Muslims are unwittingly being conditioned by their clerics and scholars to accept **SATAN** as Christ when he manifests himself to be Christ. Please keep in mind that Muslim clerics are completely in the **DARK** about how it will be **SATAN, himself,** who will be this long-expected **ANTICHRIST**. Although there are **MANY ANTICHRISTS**, the last false christ will be **SATAN**. **HE**

WILL PERSONATE JESUS CHRIST when this coming **World Federation** is established. As we have read, Muslims are also looking for a messiah to come to help them destroy **GOG** and **MAGOG**; and then, afterwards, **JESUS**, according to Muslim thinking, will kill the **DAJJAL** (ANTICHRIST). However, Bible-believing Christians will not fall for this grand delusion because they know we are to meet our **LORD in the AIR**, not here on planet Earth. Nevertheless, here is another quote from a Muslim militant website that shows what they think is going to happen shortly. Read the quote below from the website ***http://www.geocities.com/Islam2jannat/ahmed.htm***:

> *"The **last four major signs** are the appearance of **Dajjal** the individual; the appearance of the **Mahdi**, the rightly guided leader of the Muslims who will fight **Dajjal**; the re-appearance of the prophet **Jesus**, on him be peace, who as well as breaking all the crosses, killing all the pigs, marrying and having children and praying with the Muslims, will also kill **Dajjal**; and the appearance of **Juge wa ma Juge**, a tribe of people who will scatter across the world, creating destruction.*
> *"It is clear that before **Dajjal** the individual appears on earth, there must already be present and **established the system**, and the **people running that system**, which and who will support and follow him when he does appear. . . .*
> *"Amongst the descriptions of **Dajjal** in the **Hadith** collections we find the following: **Dajjal** has **ONE EYE**, like a squashed grape. . . . **Kufr** is at war with Islam. Islam is at war with Kufr. **Dajjal** will fight the **Mahdi**. The **Mahdi** will fight **Dajjal**. The **prophet Jesus**, who was not crucified, but taken by **Allah** out of this world into the Unseen, and another who looked like him crucified in his place, the prophet **Jesus**, on him be peace, having returned to this world, **will kill Dajjal**."* [sic]

Muslims teach that all the people of this world will be on **ALLAH'S side** or on the **side of the DAJJAL**. Muslims, in their blindness, call those who base their faith in the God of the Judeo-Christian Bible - "**the People of the Book**." The *KORAN* calls **JESUS "Isa"** or the son of Maryam. This following quote from the *KORAN* is one of the inscriptions that is written on the **DOME OF THE ROCK** in which its beliefs were built on a delusion that Muhammad ascended to Heaven from that spot on the Temple Mount. Let's read from Chapters 4:171; 9:30 of the *KORAN* and what it says about those who believe **JESUS** (Isa) is the Son of God:

> "*O* ***People of the book****? Commit no excesses in your religion: nor say of Allah aught but the truth.* ***Al-Masih 'Isa*** *the son of Maryam was (no more than) a messenger of Allah, and His Word, which he bestowed on* ***Maryam****, and a spirit proceeding from him: so believe in Allah and his messengers. Say not '****trinity****:' desist: it will be better for you: for Allah is one God: glory be to him: (far exalted is he) above having a* ***son****. To him belong all things in the heavens and on earth. And enough is Allah as a disposer of affairs.*
> *"The Jews call 'Uzair a son of Allah, and the Christians call* ***Al-Masih the son of Allah****.' That is a saying from their mouth; (in this) they but imitate what the unbelievers of old used to say.* ***ALLAH'S CURSE BE ON THEM****: how they are deluded away from the truth!"*

The *KORAN* teaches that, to those who believe that **JESUS** is the Son of God, "***Allah's curse be on them***." However, let's look at what the GOD of the Judeo-Christian Bible says about this in 1 John 2:22:

> "***WHO IS A LIAR BUT HE THAT DENIETH THAT JESUS IS THE CHRIST? <u>HE IS ANTICHRIST, THAT DENIETH THE FATHER AND THE SON</u>***."

Muhammad was certainly one of them. The **SAVIOUR** warned the following about the religious leaders of the Jews in **JESUS'** day, who also rejected Him as the **Son of God** and **Saviour of the world**:

> ***"I AM COME IN MY FATHER'S NAME, AND YE RECEIVE ME NOT: IF ANOTHER SHALL COME IN HIS OWN NAME, HIM YE WILL RECEIVE."***
>
> ***John 5:43***

JESUS warns here that those who reject Him as the Messiah will end up receiving these **false christs** and **false prophets** whom He foretold to come after Him in Matthew 24:23, 24:

> *"Then if any man shall say unto you, Lo, here is Christ, or there; believe it not. For there shall arise **FALSE CHRISTS**, and **FALSE PROPHETS**, and shall shew great signs and wonders; insomuch that, if it were possible, they shall deceive the very elect."*

About 500 years before **Muhammad** was born, the apostle Paul pointed out the following in 1 Corinthians 12:3:

> *"Wherefore I give you to understand, **THAT NO MAN SPEAKING BY THE SPIRIT OF GOD CALLETH JESUS ACCURSED: AND THAT NO MAN CAN SAY THAT JESUS IS THE LORD, BUT BY THE HOLY GHOST**."*

As we saw, **Muhammad** dictated to his scribes, who wrote the *KORAN*, that those who call **JESUS** the Son of God "***<u>let Allah's curse be on them</u>***." However, the apostle John also warned the following in 1 John 2:18, 22:

> *"Little children, it is the last time: and as ye have heard **<u>THAT ANTICHRIST SHALL COME</u>**, even now are **<u>THERE MANY ANTICHRISTS;</u>** whereby we know that it is the last time. Who is a **LIAR** but he that **<u>DENIETH</u>** that **<u>JESUS</u>** is the **Christ? <u>HE IS ANTICHRIST</u>**, that **<u>DENIETH</u>** the **<u>FATHER</u>** and the **<u>SON</u>**."*

Does not Islam and its founder deny that **JESUS** is the Son of God? On the next page, there are the titles of three leaders of the **three World Revolutions** that have caused most of the death and destruction to mankind since the **fall of Pagan Rome in A.D. 476**. Although the **Papacy** does not reject **JESUS** as the Son of God, its spiritual leader, the **Pope**, claims to be **Christ's Vicar on earth**, whose position only belongs to the **Holy Spirit.** The book, *Beware It's Coming -*

LATIN (ROMAN NUMERALS)
(VICAR OF THE SON OF GOD - OFFICIAL TITLE OF THE POPE OF ROME)

V	I	C	A	R	I	U	S	F	I	L	I	I	D	E	I		
5	**1**	**100**			**1**	**5**			**1**	**50**	**1**	**1**	**500**		**1**	**=**	**666**

It will be a **POPE OF ROME** who will become the future leader of this **WORLD FEDERATION** that **JESUS** calls **BABYLON THE GREAT** (Revelation 17:5), not the founder of **ISLAM** or **MAITREYA**. However, 1 John 2:18 states there are "many **ANTICHRISTS**." The last **ANTICHRIST**, however, will be Satan himself!

GREEK (MUHAMMAD)
FROM TURKISH SPELLING

M	A	O	M	E	T	I	S		
40	**1**	**70**	**40**	**5**	**300**	**10**	**200**	**=**	**666**

The false interpretation of the Book of Revelation stating the **BEAST** is a man who will be the Antichrist from the tribe of Dan of Judaism is as false as Baal Worship. The **ANTICHRIST** is **SATAN** and this **BEAST** is symbolizing his **KINGDOM** that he is working through.

HEBREW (MAITREYA)
NEW AGE MESSIAH

M	A	I	Th	R	I	E		
40	**1**	**10**	**400**	**200**	**10**	**5**	**=**	**666**

Taken From *The 21-st Century Revelation Seminar Teacher's Manual*, William Josiah Sutton

The Antichrist 666, has a more diligent study about the origin of Baal Worship and how the Papacy was foretold by the angel Gabriel as the Little Horn (Daniel 7:24, 25) and by **JESUS** as the Beast from the Sea, to whom the **DRAGON GAVE HIM HIS POWER, AND HIS SEAT, AND GREAT AUTHORITY**. (See Revelation 13:2) It is predicted in Revelation, Chapter 13, that it will be a **POPE** of the Roman Catholic Church who will become the **spiritual leader** of modern Babylon the Great in our day, not the president of the United States nor this New Age messiah named Maitreya. However, like 1 John 2:18 states, there were to be "**MANY ANTICHRISTS**," not just one. However, "**THAT ANTICHRIST**," to whom the apostle of Christ is referring here, is pointing to **SATAN HIMSELF** of whom the **POPE OF ROME** is only a shadow of the real one to come.

It is not by chance that Muhammad's name in its Turkish spelling (Mahomet), when translated into Greek, will also add to **666**. About **474 years** before **MUHAMMAD** was born in Mecca, the *BOOK OF REVELATION* foretold the founder of *ISLAM* as a ***FALLING STAR*** and the religion of ***ISLAM***, which **MUHAMMAD** and his successors spread by violence and destruction, as **PLAGUES OF ARABIAN DESERT LOCUSTS**. What was revealed about *ISLAM* in this book is only a small analysis of what ***ISLAM*** has been up to since its founding in **A.D. 610**. This writer shows in Book II of *In Gog They Trust?* a more complete study on the rise and evolution of ***ISLAM*** and how it was, indeed, foretold in Revelation, Chapter 9.

It is not by chance either that **MUHAMMAD** was foretold in Revelation 9:1 as a **FALLING STAR**. Ironically enough, *ISLAM'S* founder was also poetically symbolized in 53:1 of the *KORAN* as ***AL-NAJM***, which means "***THE STAR***," "*when it sets;*" and it is not by chance that *ISLAM* today uses the **FIVE-POINTED STAR SIGN** to symbolize both their prophet and the **FIVE PILLARS OF ISLAM**. As pointed out, thousands of years before the birth of Muhammad, the pagan Arabians in the south unwittingly worshipped **LUCIFER** as ***ATHTAR*** whose home, in his myth, was the planet **VENUS**. The Arabic name ***ATHTAR***, when translated into Latin, becomes **LUCIFER**[62] who also played the part of the **Moon-god** ***SIN*** of the Sumerians and Phoenicians and whose father in Phoenician Mythology was ***IL***, the Sky-god, to whom the title ***AL-ILAH*** (ALLAH) "***THE GOD***" traces as well.

This independent researcher brings out in Book II of *In Gog They Trust?* that **Muhammad** borrowed heavily from both the **Cabala** (also Qabalah) (Jewish Mysticism) and **Gnosticism** (Christian Mysticism) to produce the *KORAN*. As we shall see shortly, educated Muslims are discovering that Muhammad was not a prophet of the Judeo-Christian God, but a prophet of **SPIRITUALISM** a.k.a. **MYSTICISM** who cleverly wrapped **JESUS** in the mantle of the **MAGIS** of the Qabalah and the Gnostics of whom Muhammad was himself an adept.

On the other side of **Spiritualism**, there stands militant *ISLAM'S* rival, the gigantic networks of the **New Age Movement**, which is a child of **Freemasonry**, as is this **New World Order scheme**. The main leaders of the New Age Movement and the **NWO** are high-ranking **FREEMASONS** whose doctrines are rooted and grounded in the Chaldean religion of Astrology, which teaches that mankind will pass through **SEVEN AGES** after which a **christ** would come whom they call **MAITREYA**. New Agers also believe in **JESUS**, like the Muslims do. They believe Him to be a great teacher who reached perfection, but reject Him as the Son of God and Saviour of the world. New Agers believe that another **NEW AGE** is to come after the year 2000 and that **another christ**, besides **JESUS**, will come to usher it in. On the other hand, Muslims believe that this false christ will be a **JEWISH MESSIAH** and that the **FREEMASONS** are his **forerunners**.

This illustration showing how the titles of the **POPE, MAITREYA,** and the founder of ***ISLAM*** all add to **666** was also taken from the above book. In it, there is plenty of evidence that shows how American Bible-believing Christians are, indeed, caught in the middle of a **dangerous conflict** between those who are running **Freemasonry** and its **New World Order scheme** and those who are running the **Muslim Revolution**. In this book, the reader will see how the **PAPACY** and **FREEMASONRY** and the **APOSTATE PROTESTANTS** of America are presently uniting themselves together in this **New World Order** scheme, which **Muslims** are violently against. Most Masons in the United States who attend church belong to **Protestant** denominations. This above book shows how **Freemasonry**, since it arrived in America from England in the early 1700s, has been conditioning American citizens to accept **BAAL WORSHIP** via **Greek Mythology** and **Philosophy**.

Although Muslims are right in saying that Masonic revolutionaries made plans to take complete control over the world, they are not aware of how this **GREAT, RED DRAGON** is also using Muslim revolutionaries to bring about a **TIME OF TROUBLE** that never was since there was a nation. As pointed out from their own words, Muslim militants think that ***ISLAM***, after the armies of **GOG** and **MAGOG** are destroyed, will one day be the universal religion. Again, Muslim militants mistakenly believe that it is the **FREEMASONS** of Europe and America who are the modern **MAGOGITES** who are presently setting up the ***DAJJAL*** (ANTICHRIST) **SYSTEM**, which is a mixture of both truth and error. The ***JUGE WA MA JUGE***, as Muslims refer to them, are not as they stated. It is not the **WALL STREET JEWS** of New York City who are secretly behind this scheme to globalize the whole world against God and His people.

This **New World Order** scheme is not solely a **JEWISH CONSPIRACY**, as Muslims are trying to sell the whole world into believing. Again, the people who have been controlling the New Age and the New World Order Movements, since their Occult-based World Revolution first began on **May Day, 1776,** are **LUCIFERIAN** in doctrine, whose adepts are mainly Aryan racists. To prove again that Muslim clerics are completely in the **DARK** about the prophecies concerning the **ANTICHRIST**, please look at this article to your right from "**JEWS AGAINST ZIONISM**." Although this writer does not at all agree with these **JEWS AGAINST ZIONISM's** interpretation about the prophecies about the **Messiah** and has no direct connection with them, he does agree with what they are trying to say to the world about modern-day **ISRAEL**. Militant Muslims often refer to the **United States** today as the **MASONIC WEST**. Another Muslim website that a Bible-believing Christian can view to see what Muslims are up to and, at the same time, see with Muslim eyes what they think about the **MASONS**, who are presently controlling the financial and political destinies of America, is **YUSUF'S DOMAIN** which is located at ***http://members.lycos.co.uk/yusufsdomain/islamdajjal.html***.

While Muslim militants call **AMERICA "the Great Satan"** and/or the **Masonic West**, along with some other names, nevertheless, according to ***IslamReview.com,*** Muslim intellectuals are leaving *ISLAM*

JEWS AGAINST ZIONISM

THE STATE OF ISRAEL HAS DECLARED ALL-OUT WAR ON THE JEWISH PEOPLE WORLDWIDE

Ariel Sharon, the Prime Minister of Israel told the crowd at a Rome hotel. "We are witness to a great wave of anti-Semitism, and apart from the usual anti-Semitism against Jews, there is today the added hate of the collective Jew, which is Israel."... "The best solution to anti-Semitism is immigration to Israel. It is the only place on Earth where Jews can live as Jews," he said. (BBC website of Monday, 17 November, 2003 (http://news.bbc.co.uk/1/hi/world/middle_east/3275979.stm)

Mr. Sharon has moved from the planning stages as stated in November, 2003, to the execution of the plan which has been in development since the days of Herzl, the founder of the Zionist movement, who stated in his diary "It is essential that the sufferings of Jews. . . become worse. . . this will assist in realization of our plans. . .I have an excellent idea. . . I shall induce anti-Semites to liquidate Jewish wealth. . . The anti-Semites will assist us thereby in that they will strengthen the persecution and oppression of Jews. The anti-Semites shall be our best friends". (From his Diary, Part I, pp. 16)

In executing this plan they have successfully escalated anti-Semitism throughout the world.
There is great pain that the press and politicians are calling the actions of the Zionist movement "Jewish actions." With these words they are helping the Zionists to fulfill their dreams.
We call upon the world again to understand that the state of "Israel" does not represent the Jewish faith and traditions and that Zionists are the greatest enemies to the Jewish people.

We appeal to people of good will in the media itself to open their minds and hearts to what we are proclaiming about the truth of Judaism, which has been distorted by the Zionists.

The promises of the Torah are always to be realized. This verse from the Torah demonstrates that those who are his enemies will pay a price when The kingdom of G-D will prevail.

Deuteronomy 32:43: Praise his People, O Nations: For he will avenge the blood of his servants. He will render vengeance against his adversaries and make expiation for his land and his People.

by the thousands every day. Educated Muslims have not only discovered for themselves the outright falsehoods found in *ISLAM,* but also how its teachings are inconsistent with science, logic, human rights, and ethics. According to Ali Sina's article in *Islam Review,* "this is the beginning of a mass exodus from Islam." He said: "It is a movement that is already in motion and nothing can stop it."[63]

In Revelation, Chapter 16, it foretold that **THREE WORLD POWERS** in the **Time of the End** would **globalize the whole world** into what **JESUS** called in Revelation 17:5 "**BABYLON THE GREAT, THE MOTHER OF HARLOTS AND ABOMINATIONS OF THE EARTH**." In the book, *Ancient Prophecies About The Dragon, The Beast, and The False Prophet*, there is overwhelming evidence that identifies these **THREE WORLD POWERS**, which are forming modern-day BABYLON today, as the **PEOPLE OF NEW AGE SPIRITUALISM, THE PAPACY,** and the **APOSTATE PROTESTANTS OF AMERICA** who are very busy today in trying to unite the whole world under the banner of the **UNITED NATIONS**.

Both Daniel the prophet of the Old Testament and the apostle John of the New Testament were shown that **SATAN'S** final plans are to move his headquarters from the **VATICAN to ISRAEL** where he will finally come to his end in this present world. However, just before the **GOD** of the Judeo-Christian Bible brings modern Babylon to nothing, like He did during the time of Nimrod, this same **GOD** who destroyed the Pharaoh and his mighty army in the days of Moses is giving **Jews**, **Catholics**, **Muslims**, and all those who have ensnared themselves with these various pagan religions of ancient and **modern Spiritualism** a chance to separate themselves from them before the Lord utterly destroys those who remain. The whole world is slowly, but surely, being globalized into joining the **United Nations**. All the people of **New Age Spiritualism**, the **Roman Catholic Church**, and the **apostate Protestants** are mingling themselves with the seed of men via the **United Nations**. This Masonic-based **modern Tower of Babel** is what the **Rothschild** and **Rockefeller Families** used to establish modern Israel in **1948**. All this is fully documented in *The Real Truth About UFOS and The New World Order Connection.* Please read to your right the quotes from the Bible and also **David Ben Gurion's** statement about the **UN**. The **United Nations** is the **FREEMASONS' Trojan Horse**!

United Nations' photograph taken by Wil Sutton

"And he shall plant the tabernacles of his ***PALACE*** *between the* ***SEAS*** *in the* ***GLORIOUS HOLY MOUNTAIN****; yet he shall* ***COME TO HIS END****, and none shall help him."*

Daniel 11:45

"With the exception of the U.S.S.R. as a federated state, all other countries ***will be united in a world alliance*** *at whose disposal will be an* ***international police force****. All armies will be abolished and there will be no more wars. In* ***JERUSALEM*** *the* ***UNITED NATIONS*** *(a truly United Nations) will* ***build a shrine*** *to the prophets to serve* ***the federated union of all continents****. This will be the* ***SEAT OF THE SUPREME COURT OF MANKIND*** *to settle all controversies* ***among the federated continents****, as prophesied by Isaiah."*

Look magazine, January 16, 1962, David ben Gurion

"In stage III (of Disarmanent) progressive controlled disarmament . . . would proceed to a point where ***no state would have the military power*** *to challenge the progressively strengthened* ***UN PEACE FORCE*** *and all international disputes would be settled according to agreed principles of international conduct . . . . The peace-keeping capabilities of the* ***UNITED NATIONS*** *would be suffficiently strong and the obligations of all states under such arrangements sufficiently far-reaching as to assure peace and the just settlement of differences in a* ***DISARMED WORLD****."*

Department of State Publication 7277
quoted in The Rockefeller File, Gary Allen, p. 89

My Jewish and Muslim reader, back in 1970, this writer was not a believer in the Judeo-Christian Bible nor in Jesus Christ as the Son of the Living God, as well. Although there are some mistranslations and typographical errors in the Kings James Version of the Bible, nevertheless, it was the combination of **Bible prophecy** from this **Judeo-Christian Bible** and the **Science of Archaeology** that proved to this great sinner that there is a **GOD** who has a **SON**, and as predicted from the Old Testament prophets, He died for the sins of all of us. My Jewish and Muslim reader, have you ever thought about putting away all your **preconceived opinions** about **JESUS** and just trying yourself to disprove the prophecies of Moses and the prophets found in the Judeo-Christian Bible? You cannot because the prophets of the Old Testament were amazingly **100% accurate** in predicting future events in history. We live in a time that we can check out these Hebrew prophets to see if their predictions failed or not. It is the same thing about the predictions from Moses to Malachi about the coming **Messiah**, whom the prophet Isaiah clearly said was the Son of God. (See Isaiah 9:6)

In the book, *Beware It's Coming-The Antichrist 666*, I gathered as many of the prophecies about the promised Messiah that I could find in the Old Testament, and then I compared them side by side with what was recorded in the New Testament for my Jewish and Muslim reader to see for themselves. I was amazed to see how **JESUS** fulfilled every prophecy about the **promised Messiah** given by Moses to Malachi! This same **JESUS** prophesied these things written to your right, and it was **He** who gave the apostles in the New Testament the warning about the **Antichrist** centuries before there was a Khazar Jew or Muslim. All those who reject **Jesus Christ** as the **Son of God** and **Saviour** of the world will, indeed, end up on the side of the **ANTICHRIST**. It was the **angel Gabriel** who showed **Daniel the prophet** the very year of Christ's **BAPTISM** in **A.D. 27** and also His **CRUCIFIXION** in **A.D. 31**, which **Muhammad** falsely said never happened. All this was clearly predicted in Daniel, Chapter 9. Unfortunately, both the prophets of the Old Testament and the apostles in the New Testament predicted that most of the people of this present world will, like the **Jews** in **JESUS'** day, **reject Him** as the **Messiah** and **Saviour of the world**. However, all those who obey the **Gospel Call** will leave these faiths who reject Him and will join those who keep God's Commandments and have the Faith of Jesus!

*"***I AM HE*** that* ***liveth****, and* ***was dead****; and, behold,* ***I am alive for evermore****. Amen; and have the* ***keys of hell*** *and of* ***death****."*

Revelation 1:18

*"***All*** that the* ***Father giveth me shall come to me****; and* ***him that cometh to me I will in no wise cast out****.*

*"***No man*** can come to me,* ***except the Father*** *which hath sent me* ***draw him****: and* ***I will raise him up at the last day****.*

"It is written in the prophets, And ***they shall be all taught of God****.* ***Every man*** *therefore that* ***hath heard****, and* ***hath learned of the Father, cometh unto me****."*

John 6:37, 44, 45

FOOTNOTE SOURCES

1. Page 9 *Encyclopedia of Occultism and Parapsychology*, Vol.1, Gale Research Company, 1978, p. 460
2. Page 9 *Occult Illustrated Dictionary*, Harvey Day, Kay &Ward London, Oxford University Press, NY, 1976, pp. 56, 57
3. Page 9 *Ibid.*, p. 57
4. Page 11 *Joy of Sects*, Occhiogrosso, Doubleday, NY, 1994, p.64, 65
5. Page 11 *Maitreya Ad* from Tara Press, London, 1982
6. Page 13 http://www.666beast.com/
7. Page 13 *Beware It's Coming - The Antichrist 666*, Sutton p. 142
8. Page 13 http://www.-answering-christianity.com/jesus_in_ islam.htm
9. Page 14 http://www.royalty.nu/Europe/England/Stuart/James1.html
10. Page14 http://www.heart7.net/knights-templar-conspiracy.htm
11. Page15 http://www.muslimsonline.com/babri/yajujmajuj.htm
12. Page15 http://www.islam.tc/prophecies/masdaj.html
13. Page15 http://members.lycos.co.uk/yusufsdomain/usaseal.html
14. Page16 http://oregonstate.edu/instruct/phl302/philosophers/bacon.html
15. Page 16 *Sunday Visitor*, November 15, 1914
16. Page 16 http://www.ordotempli.org/the_merovingians.htm
17. Page 16 *Beware It's Coming - The Antichrist 666*, Sutton, p.137
18. Page 19 http://www.cnn.com/2003/US/Northeast/12/19/wtc.plan
19. Page 19 *The New Age Movement and The Illuminati 666*, Sutton, The Institute of Religious Knowledge, 1983, pp. 70-73
20. Page 19 http://www.freemasonry-org.il/scottish.html
21. Page 28 Wainright House Guide, Fall/Winter 1990
22. Page 29 http://www.fordham.edu/halsall/source/732tours.html
23. Page 29 http://www.geocities.com/islam2jannat/ahmed.htm
24. Page 30 *An Encyclopaedia of Freemasonry and Its Kindred Sciences*, Vol. 1, Mackey 33°, p. 368
25. Page 31 http://www.islam.tc/prophecies/masdaj.html
26. Page 32 http://allaahuakbar.net/free-masons/index.htm
27. Page 32 http://www.missionislam.com/nwo/index/.htm
28. Page 36 *The Great Controversy*, White, 1888, p. 624
29. Page 37 http://allaahuakbar.net/free-masons/dajjal.htm
30. Page 37 http://www.inter-islam.org/faith/dajjal/.htm

31. Page 41 http://www.streetswing.com/histmain/z3maypol.htm
32. Page 43 http://nabataea.net/dushares.html
33. Page 45 *The New Age Movement and The Illuminati 666*, p. 139
34. Page 47 *The Real Truth About UFOs and the New World Order Connection*, Sutton, pp. 34-37
35. Page 48 http://www.britannia.com/history/bb1312.html
36. Page 48 http://www.lundyisleofavalon.co.uk/templars/tempic11.htm
37. Page 49 http:www.islam.com/reply.asp?id=450161&ct=6&mn=450161
38. Page 51 *Young's Analytical Concordance*, Young, p.66
39. Page 51 *Mythology of All Races*, Gray, Vol. 5, pp. 5-7
40. Page 51 *A Dictionary of World Mythology*, Cotterell, p. 66
41. Page 52 *Ibid.*, p. 66
42. Page 52 http://www.meem.freeuk.com/Kalima.html
43. Page 52 http:www.islamreview.com/articles/theroad.shtml
44. Page 52 http://www.sacredsites.com/middle_east/saudi_arabia/mecca.html
45. Page 53 www.bible.ca/islam/islam-myths-hajj-pagan-origin.htm
46. Page 65 www.geocities.com/islam2jannat/ahmed.htm
47. Page 65 www.islamicaweb.com/archive/read/t-26441
48. Page 66 www.islamicparty.com/commonsense/14gog.htm
49. Page 66 http://www..geocities.com/atid10/mainbb.htm
50. Page 66 www.biblebelievers.org.au/13trib02.htm#Conversion
51. Page 67 http://www.fact-index.com/k.kh/khazars.html
52. Page 68 http://www.informationblast.com/Derbent.html
53. Page 69 www.fact-index.com/g/go/gog.html
54. Page 71 *Young's Concordance to the Bible*, Young, p. 8
55. Page 72 http://www.hostkingdom.net/siberia.html
56. Page 72 *Ibid.*
57. Page 73 www.geocities.com/jewishwarriors/critkhaz.html
58. Page 73 http:www.stormfront.org/whitehistory/hwr31.htm
59. Page 74 http://www.hostkingdom.net/iran.html#Parni
60. Page 74 http://www.silk-road.com/artl/heph.shtml
61. Page 74 *The Encyclopedia Americana*, Vol. 2, 1975, p. 436
62. Page 84 *The New Age Movement and The Illuminati*, Sutton, p. 70
63.Page 88 http://islamreview.com/articles/fastdemise.shtml

This volume is a prophetical, archaeological, and historical study into the prophecies about Christ and the Antichrist. Its documented pages are loaded with plenty of evidence to prove to the Jew, Muslim, and New Ager that Jesus of Nazareth is the Son of God and the promised Messiah. However, it shows without mixing words how mainstream Christianity has apostatized from the faith once delivered to the saints. It plainly shows its reader how to tell the difference between Christ and the Antichrist and where we can find the origin of the number 666 and who is branded with it today.

This volume is centered around the prophecies about the Beast from the Bottomless Pit and Occult-based secret societies, like Freemasonry, and how both the New Age and the New World Order Movements derived out of the Masonic World Revolution that was first launched on May Day, 1776. While the above book shows the spiritual side of this spirit of Antichrist, this volume exposes its more political side. It takes its reader through the rise and evolution of the Illuminati and the dangerous secret societies in America who are its offshoots.

This volume examines the **UFO** phenomenon and with overwhelming evidence from Bible prophecy proves that it is **SATAN**, not **JESUS**, who is preparing to move the headquarters of his invisible **KINGDOM** to Israel. The author shows how the founding of modern-day Israel is one grand delusion of the Antichrist and how both Jews and mainstream Christians are being conditioned to receive him as their long-expected messiah. It was the House of Rothschild, not the Biblical God, who first established modern Israel. See how the **UN** is the **SEAT** of the **NWO** and how it was planned to move the **UN** headquarters from New York to **ISRAEL**.

This volume is a comprehensive study about Revelation, Chapter 9, and how Jesus through His apostle John foretold Muhammad as a falling star, to whom Muslims today poetically refer in the Koran as Al-Najm. It also covers the history of the American-based Nation of Islam and its origin. This volume also shows how Freemasonry is a counterfeit of Islam and how Mormonism is a counterfeit of Freemasonry by using their own words. This fully-documented volume also shows how the rivaling Papacy, Muslims, Freemasons, Mormons, and New Age Socialists all used the Entertainment Field as their revolutionary weapon in their own individual efforts to bring the whole world under their subordination.

This volume is centered around the Loud Cry of the Third Angel, which is found in Revelation, Chapters 14 and 18. This is the most solemn warning ever given by this world's True God. Its warning is against the coming World Federation, which Jesus called Babylon the Great (Revelation 17:5), and these **three world powers** symbolized as the Dragon, the Beast, and the False Prophet that are presently forming modern Babylon today. This volume is fully documented and has many illustrations and diagrams and identifies, with overwhelming evidence, just who these three world powers are today who are forming modern Babylon.

Book 1 of *In Gog They Trust?* shows from their own words how Muslim militants believe today that it is the Order of the Freemasons that is secretly behind the New World Order (NWO) and that the NWO is the Antichrist System which was foretold to come shortly before the Antichrist (Dajjal) appears. This volume shows with plenty of documented evidence how Muslim clerics are teaching that it is the Freemasons who are secretly controlling both European and American governments and that it is Europe and America who are Gog and Magog. The author shows with plenty of documented facts how, indeed, Bible-believing Christians today are caught up in a dangerous and bloody struggle between the NWO advocates and the Muslim militants over who is going to control Israel and the world. The author also shows how this NWO is not a Khazarian Jewish scheme, as Muslims erroneously believe, but a Luciferian plot, and that the Zionists, the Muslims, and the advocates for the NWO have **NO** Biblical or lawful right to control the Holy Land that they are all fighting over.

Book II of *In Gog They Trust*? picks up where Book I of *In Gog They Trust?* left off. It shows how the Judeo-Christian God foretold the Roman Catholic, Muslim, and Masonic Revolutions and how they are responsible for most of the death and carnage among mankind since the Fall of the Western Roman Empire in A.D. 476. This volume shows how the sure Word of prophecy foretold that it will be the various divisions of modern-day Spiritualism (Paganism), the Papacy, and the American Protestant **RULING CLASS**, who belong to Occult-based secret societies, that will establish this coming Antichrist System which the Biblical Jesus called Babylon the Great. The author shows how both the Roman Catholic and Protestant churches were subtly transformed into being **INTERFAITH CHURCHES** by the infiltration of Freemasonry in preparation for this coming merger of all religions and nations *via* the United Nations, the modern Tower of Babel.

Sim & Sons' Publishing House
10624 S. Eastern Avenue, Suite A #177
Henderson, NV 89052

ORDER FORM

TITLE	UNIT PRICE
Beware It's Coming - The Antichrist 666	$11.00
The New Age Movement and The Illuminati 666	$11.00
The Real Truth About UFOs and The New World Order Connection	$11.00
Ancient Prophecies About Mysticism, Hollywood, and The Music Industry	$12.00
Ancient Prophecies About The Dragon, The Beast, and The False Prophet	$12.00
In Gog They Trust?, Book I	$10.00
In Gog They Trust?, Book II (still under construction)	$12.00

TO ORDER, PLEASE CALL OUR TOLL-FREE NUMBER

1-866-899-1877

SUNDAY-THURSDAY 9-9
PLUS POSTAGE & HANDLING

Allow 3 - 6 weeks delivery

Also visit our website

www.18441888.com